JULIAN GRESS subscribes
and Shorter Catechisms, For
rectories of Family and Public
Solemn League.

MW00811617

Christ Condemned

On the Incarnation
and the Trinity

Julian Gress

All Scripture quotations taken from the King James Version of the Bible.

Cover design by Dissect Designs.

ISBN
978-1-950436-00-2 (paperback)
978-1-950436-01-9 (hardback)
978-1-950436-02-6 (ebook)

Library of Congress Control Number: 2019901892

First printing edition 2019.

Julian Gress
Lynnwood, WA
julianrgress@gmail.com

to the most beautiful among women

TABLE OF CONTENTS

Christ Condemned

PREFACE

This book arose from my reading of Immanuel Kant. The imprint of that philosopher may be found throughout. Much of the book is an original exposition of his three critiques. However, the premise of the work is to apply the critical philosophy to theology, in particular, to the doctrines of the Incarnation and the Trinity. Kant argues that the existence of God is a necessary postulate of practical reason. Man must believe in God to be happy in doing his duty. In this book I argue that, on the supposition, man has sinned, the Incarnation and the Trinity are necessary postulates of practical reason, not for man to continue in his duty, but to repent of his sin. These doctrines are therefore established on the same basis that Kant established the existence of God.

Julian Gress, 2019

INTRODUCTION

Doctrines through which salvation is possible are fundamental;[1] actual, historical;[2] necessary, derivative.[3] The moral law teaches man how to persevere in original righteousness. The fundamentals of the law are the immortality of the soul, the freedom of the will, and the existence of God.[4] But the wrath of God is upon fallen man. How is it possible for God, who does not change, through the very same law that destroys sinners, also to save them? The end of grace is that of the law: charity, charity alone. Grace remedies the fall; grace brings man out of sin and death, into righteousness and life. Salvation must therefore be lawful, and lawfully conceived, to be lawfully received by fallen man.

The purpose of this work is to prove that Jesus Christ is both God and man, and that in the unity of the divine nature there are three persons, the Father, the Son, and the Holy Spirit; that the Incarnation and the Trinity are fundamental doctrines of the Christian faith, conditions of the possibility of salvation, without which no man can be saved.

Theology is the knowledge of God. The Incarnation is the constitutive principle of theology, the condition for intuiting the divine nature; the Trinity is the regulative principle of theology, the condition for thinking the divine nature intuited.[5] Each principle divides into two headings, formal and material, and each heading forms three moments, thesis, antithesis, and synthesis.[6] There are therefore twelve fundamental doctrines of revealed religion, to be proven in the work itself.[7]

---

[1] Matt. 16:13-28; John 8:24; 1 John 2:20-24, 4:1-6, 5:1-21; 2 John 7-10.

[2] John 1:14; 1 Cor. 15; Gal. 4:4-5; Matt. 16:21-23; 2 Pet. 1:16-21; Acts 17:30-31, 18:24-28, 19.

[3] Rom. 6, 8:28-39; Gal. 4:6, 5:4; Heb. 9:14; Eph. 2:1-10.

[4] Immanuel Kant, *Critique of Pure Reason*, trans. by Werner S. Pluhar (Indianapolis: Hackett Publishing Company, 1996), Bxxix-Bxxxiii, B377-396, B697-736, B825-B858; Immanuel Kant, *Critique of Practical Reason*, ed. by Mary Gregor, trans. by Mary Gregor (Cambridge: Cambridge University Press, 1997), 5:28-30, 5:122-132. The ideas of pure reason, according to Kant.

[5] *Pure Reason*, B110, B220-223, B692.

[6] Klaus Reich, *The Completeness of Kant's Table of Judgments*, ed. by Eckart Forster, trans. by Jane Kneller and Michael Losonsky (Stanford: Stanford University Press 1992), 103-108. I use the triad here in a Kantian sense, to be explained throughout.

[7] The form of this work closely follows Kant, especially his *Metaphysical Foundations of Natural Science*, ed. by Michael Friedman, trans. by Michael Friedman (Cambridge: Cambridge University Press, 2004).

What has hitherto been called systematic theology is not truly systematic, but organized, bringing certain doctrines under headings without explicating them according to the unity of the whole.[8] Fundamental doctrine pertains to the Father; this is the foundation of the system of theology. Historical doctrine pertains to the manifestation of the Son of God in history; derivative doctrine to the application of Christ's work to the church by the Holy Spirit. I reserve their exposition to two future works, if the Lord wills it.

---

[8] Kant, *Pure Reason*, B89-92, B106-107, B860-863.

PART I—THE INCARNATION

SECTION 1—THE NATURE OF GOD

Definition

God is an inwardly lawful being.[1] An inwardly lawful being is one whose righteousness and blessedness are identical. Righteousness is lawfulness, blessedness is the union of lawfulness and happiness, and their identity is holiness.

Man is an outwardly lawful being of sensible intuition[2]; an angel, of intellectual intuition. An outwardly lawful being is one whose righteousness and blessedness are distinct.

Proposition

There is a God.

Proof

Man is an outwardly lawful being; his blessedness is distinct from his righteousness. Therefore, the blessedness of his righteousness depends upon a being for whom these are the same, in whom man wills his own happiness lawfully. This being is God. Therefore, God exists.[3]

Scripture Proof

Shalt thou reign, because thou closest *thyself* in cedar? did not thy father eat and drink, and do judgment and justice, *and* then *it* was

---

[1] Deut. 4:12-13, 5:24; Ps. 40:8, 51:6; Jer. 31:33; Ez. 1:4.

[2] Kant, *Critique of Pure Reason*, B33. "Intuition" is here used in the Kantian sense, as the immediate representation of an object, to be rigorously defined at length.

[3] *Pure Reason*, B832-B859; *Practical Reason*, 5:124-5:132; Immanuel Kant, *Critique of Judgment*, trans. by Werner S. Pluhar (Indianapolis: Hackett Publishing Company, 1987), ak. 447-453; Immanuel Kant, "Religion within the boundaries of mere reason," in *Religion and Rational Theology*, ed. by Allen W. Wood and George di Giovanni, trans. by George di Giovanni (New York: Cambridge University Press, 1996), 6:6-6:8. This is the author's version of Kant's moral argument for the existence of God. Kant presents his proof in various ways, but always includes the union of morality and happiness.

well with him? He judged the cause of the poor and needy; then *it was* well *with him:* was not this to know me? saith the LORD. Jeremiah 22:15-16

To do one's duty, and be happy for it, this is the knowledge of God.

Come, ye children, hearken unto me: I will teach you the fear of the LORD. What man *is he that* desireth life, *and loveth* many days, that he may see good? Keep thy tongue from evil, and thy lips from speaking guile. Depart from evil, and do good; seek peace, and pursue it. The eyes of the LORD *are* upon the righteous, and his ears *are open* unto their cry. The face of the LORD *is* against them that do evil, to cut off the remembrance of them from the earth. Psalm 34:11-16

Scripture proves God's perfect righteousness from his necessary work.

Shall not the Judge of all the earth do right? Genesis 18:25

Therefore hearken unto me, ye men of understanding: far be it from God, *that he should do* wickedness; and *from* the Almighty, *that he should commit* iniquity. For the work of a man shall he render unto him, and cause every man to find according to *his* ways. Yea, surely God will not do wickedly, neither will the Almighty pervert judgment. Job 34:10-12

Is God unrighteous who taketh vengeance? (I speak as a man) God forbid: for then how shall God judge the world? Romans 3:5-6

See also Deut. 30:11-16; Ps. 1, 37, 58, 125; Prov. 8:32-36, 24:19-20; Jer. 9:6, 23-24; Hos. 6:6; Mal. 3:13-18; Col. 1:9-10; Is. 1:19-20, 3:10-11, 35; Rom. 1:18-21, 2:12-17; Eph. 6:1-8; Heb. 11:1-6; Jas. 1:22-25.

Comment

The moral law is a concept that contains within itself the ground of an intuition; the universal concept of the moral law is *the concept of the ground of an intuition.* The moral law is the conceptualization of grounds, or groundedness in concepts.[4] It commands through its form, without the matter, unconditionally.[5]

Man desires happiness.[6] Happiness is the agreement of the will with its object.[7] If man wills an object, he wills pleasure in the actuality of the object willed.[8] The law is the universal form of the will; happiness, the particular, is its matter.[9]

Man ought to obey the law, and he also desires happiness; therefore, the end of man is the union of lawfulness and happiness.[10] This is blessedness.[11] The concept of this union is singular, and the singular is the form of an intuition.

The moral law contains within itself the ground of an intuition in agreement with its concept. The concept of the law is righteousness, and its intuition is blessedness. Righteousness is to be the ground of blessedness, and blessedness must be willed righteously, and must itself be righteous;[12] but being not righteous in itself, there is one in whom it is, who is holy.[13] This union is a concept with its intuition, a being, and this being is God.[14]

---

[4] Ex. 20:1-17; Deut. 5:6-21; 30:11-14; Ps. 119:11, 89, 96, 130, 142, 152, 160; Immanuel Kant, *Groundwork of the Metaphysics of Morals*, ed. by Mary Gregor, trans. by Mary Gregor (Cambridge: Cambridge University Press, 1998), 4:389, 4:402; *Practical Reason*, 5:27.

[5] Gen. 3:11, 17; Num. 14:40-45; Deut. 4:6; 1 Sam. 13:8-14; 2 Sam. 6:6-7; 1 Kings 13:20-26; Job 28; Ps. 19:7-10, 90:3, 119:140; Is. 35:8-10; *Practical Reason* 5:15-5:41; *Groundwork*, 4:416-445.

[6] Gen. 30:1, 49:15; Num. 11:4-6; Ps. 34:12; *Practical Reason*, 5:22, 25; *Groundwork*, 4:415-416.

[7] Gen. 30:13; *Pure Reason*, B834; *Practical Reason*, 5:22; 5:124.

[8] Deut. 21:11; Prov. 13:19; Ecc. 6:9; *Judgment*, ak. 209, 206'.

[9] *Practical Reason*, 5:19-41.

[10] Ps. 1, 15, 16, 20, 21, 23, 91, 128; *Pure Reason*, B841-842; *Practical Reason*, 5:107-113.

[11] A blessing is a good word. A word is an image of a concept, a sensible representation distinct from the concept, as the Son is both the word and image of God. Therefore, blessedness is the union of goodness (lawfulness) and happiness in intuition.

[12] Ps. 1:1-2; Is. 32:17; Jas. 1:25; *Practical Reason*, 5:113-119.

[13] Gen. 1:3, 10, 12, 18, 21-22, 25, 28, 31, 2:3; Ps. 85:10; Jer. 17:5-13; Matt. 5:3-12, 5:8 with Heb. 12:14; Jas. 1:25; Rev. 20:6. These three, righteousness, blessedness, and holiness, may be found together in various passages of Scripture, especially the Psalms.

[14] *Pure Reason*, B74-76, B124-126, A103-110, B272-274, B423, B620-630; Aristotle, *Metaphysics* 1029a27-31, 1032a12-14, 1033b19-26, 1036a2-9. Without a concept to recognize the intuition, nothing exists. I do not say, without a thinking subject, for although the concept inheres in the thinking subject, it subsists also in the object, like as subject to predicate, as particular condition of its being.

God is happy in righteousness, and therefore perfectly righteous, and being perfectly happy in his own perfect righteousness, whatsoever God wills necessarily comes to pass.[15] In willing God's will, man wills his own happiness lawfully, and receives the reward of his obedience from a holy lawgiver and judge.[16]

Proposition 1

There is one God.

Proof

The blessedness of the divine nature is identical to its righteousness. The blessedness of God is his intuition, his righteousness is his concept, and the intuition of God is identical to his concept. The concept of the divine nature is one; therefore, the intuition of God is also one, and the being of God, the intuition in agreement with the concept, is one, that is, there is one God.[17]

Scripture Proof

> And God spake all these words, saying, I *am* the LORD thy God, which have brought thee out of the land of Egypt, out of the house of bondage. Thou shalt have no other gods before me. Exodus 20:1-2, cf. Deut. 5:6-7

---

[15] Gen. 1:3-4, etc.; Ps. 33:4-11, 115:3; Prov. 8; Is. 43:13; Jer. 10:12-13; Heb. 1:3, 11:3; Rev. 4:11.

[16] Ruth 2:12; 1 Sam. 24:19; 2 Sam. 3:39; 1 Chron. 28:9; Ps. 7:9; Is. 40:10; Jer. 17:10; Hos. 4:9; Obad. 1:15; 2 Tim. 4:14; Rev. 2:23; Kant, *Pure Reason,* B842; *Practical Reason,* 5:140. Hence the efficacy of prayer.

[17] *Pure Reason,* B604; Immanuel Kant, "Lectures on the philosophical doctrine of religion," in *Religion and Rational Theology*, ed. by Allen W. Wood and George di Giovanni, trans. by Allen W. Wood (New York: Cambridge University Press, 1996), 28:1027, B604; Aristotle, *Metaphysics* 1034a32-39; Thomas Aquinas, *Summa Theologica* 11.3. The concepts of things are unities, by the pure application of the category. The law of non-contradiction is founded on nothing else.

I am the LORD thy God, which have brought thee out of the land of Egypt, out of the house of bondage, then follows the commandment, *Thou shalt have no other gods before me,* for that he is holy, he is one.

> There is one lawgiver, who is able to save and to destroy. James 4:12

He is not a doer of the law, as though bound by it, but a judge (Jas. 4:11).

> and *there is* no God else beside me; a just God and a Saviour; *there is* none beside me. Isaiah 45:21

See also Ex. 15:11; Deut. 4:6-8, 32-40, 6:4-5, 32:4, 12; 1 Sam. 2:2; 2 Sam. 7:18-29; 1 Kings 8:23-24; 1 Chron. 17:16-27; 2 Chron. 6:14-15; Is. 42:8, 43:10-13, 44:6-8, 45:1-8, 18, 22, 46:4-5; Eph. 4:1-6; 1 Cor. 8:1-6; 1 Tim. 6:13-16; John 17:3-4.

Comment

A concept is a *universal* presentation common to several other representations; these other representations are *particular.*[18] A *singular* concept is the universal thought of as particular.[19] The particular is thought through the universal, in distinction therefrom; therefore, the particular is thought, as a concept, in the singular, wherein the universal and the particular are identified. This union, distinguished from the universal through the particular, is the form of an intuition.[20]

An object whose intuition is identical to its concept is a thing in itself, or noumenon.[21] An object whose intuition is distinct from its intuition is an appearance, or phenomenon.[22]

---

[18] Kant, *Critique of Pure Reason*, B133-134; Immanuel Kant, *Logic,* trans. by Robert S. Hartman and Wolfgang Schwarz (Mineola: Dover Publications, 1974), Section 1; Reich, *The Completeness of Kant's Table of Judgments,* 32-38; Aristotle, *Metaphysics* 1034a5-8.

[19] Kant, *Pure Reason,* B39-40, B47-48, B96-98; *Logic,* Section 21; Aristotle, *Metaphysics* 1029a27-31, 1033a23-1034a8, 1036a2-9 with 1003a-12-14; Reich, *Completeness,* 103, 105-108.

[20] Kant, *Pure Reason,* B39-40, B47-48, B96-98. Or the concept of an intuition.

[21] *Pure Reason,* B42-45, B49-72, B294-315; Reich, *Completeness,* 34-37.

[22] Gen. 1:1; Col. 1:16; Kant, *Pure Reason,* B33-36, B59-76, B294-315; Reich, *Completeness,* 32-34.

Angels identify the universal and the singular.[23] This is intellectual intuition. An angel intuits a being through its concept; therefore, angels see God.[24] Angels are unities,[25] rulers of concepts.[26]

Man distinguishes the singular from the universal. This is called sensible intuition. The universal and the singular are identical in form, distinct in matter. If, then, an intuition is given, its matter, or particularity, is thought through sensation, its form, which is its universality, is thought through concepts, and the concepts applied to the intuition yield concepts of an object, distinct from the subject and its thought.[27] The quantity of concepts is universal, particular, and singular.[28] An intuition universal is *unity*; an intuition particular is *plurality*; an intuition singular, the identity of the former, is *totality*.[29]

The unity of intuition is either conceptual or intuitive.[30] The conceptual unity is pure. It refers neither to the singular, nor to the particular, but to the universal; therefore, this unity negates all plurality. Space is the form of outer intuition,[31] and is one; there is one universal space, and all particular spaces are contained within it.[32] Time is likewise one,[33] and the world itself.[34]

The intuitive unity is empirical. Sensible intuition distinguishes the singular from the universal, therefore also the particular in the singular. The universal concept is the common unity of diverse particulars, which are distinguished from one another through their common distinction from the universal concept. Thus, empirical unity affirms the universal concept

---

[23] Aquinas, *Summa* 50.1-2, 58.1-4.

[24] Matt. 18:10; *Summa* 54.1-56.3.

[25] *Summa* 50.4.

[26] Job 38:6-7; Ps. 92:4-5, 104:4; Ez. 28:12; John 8:44; 2 Cor. 10:3-6; Eph. 6:10-13; Gal. 3:19; Rev. 21:17; Kant, *Pure Reason*, B368-396, B595-611. Plato's forms, subsisting in persons; and Aristotle's simple movers, spiritualized. It is a common idea in mythology and fantasy, where each god has a peculiar domain, and spiritual beings rule over certain abstract concepts.

[27] *Pure Reason*, B102-106. The categories.

[28] *Pure Reason*, B95; *Logic*, Section 21.

[29] *Pure Reason*, B106.

[30] *Pure Reason*, B1-B3. A priori or a posteriori.

[31] *Pure Reason*, B42.

[32] *Pure Reason*, B39.

[33] *Pure Reason*, B47, B49-51.

[34] Immanuel Kant, *Opus Postumum*, ed. by Eckart Forster, trans. by Eckart Forster and Michael Rosen (New York: Cambridge University Press, 1993), 22:115-116, 49, 21:30, 40.

in the plurality of intuition. There are many particular spaces, and of many a common measure.

Is then the unity of God pure, or empirical?

The blessedness of God is identical to his righteousness. Righteousness is the concept of the divine nature; blessedness is its intuition; therefore, the intuition of God is identical to his concept, and God is as his concept, one.

God is an inwardly lawful being. In any judgment of quantity, I am aware of the same presentation as belonging to a multitude of other presentations. When I count my fingers, I think in each what is common to all, and each one outside the others, but God is an inwardly lawful being. The divine nature cannot be intuited outside of itself, in another, but only within itself and its concept. God is therefore one.

Proposition 2

God is invisible.

Proof

Plurality is particularity thought through unity. Sensible intuition distinguishes intuitions from concepts. It conceives of intuitions as particular in relation to concepts, whereby the particular is thought through the unity of intuition. God is an inwardly lawful being. The intuition of the divine nature is identical to its concept, a conception that excludes all particularity and therefore also all plurality from the divine nature. Therefore, God cannot be represented as a plurality, or as an object of sensible intuition.[35] God is invisible.

Scripture Proof

> Thou shalt not make unto thee any graven image, or any likeness *of any thing* that *is* in heaven above, or that *is* in the earth beneath, or that *is* in the water under the earth. Exodus 20:4

---

[35] Kant, *Pure Reason*, B202-218. All sensible intuitions are extensive and intensive magnitudes.

Thou shalt not make unto thee any graven image, or any likeness, any visible representation of the divine nature; *of anything that is in heaven above, or in the earth
below, or in the waters under the earth*, all things visible, in every division of
space.

The unity of God therefore *negates plurality* in God, whether *internal*
through *division* of its space, *external* through its *multiplication,* or *material*
through the filling of space. These sins are expressly condemned by Scripture. The system of idolatry imputes physical properties to the divine nature, and traverses the path of mathematics and natural science.

> Thus saith the LORD the King of Israel, and his redeemer the
> LORD of hosts; I *am* the first, and I *am* the last; and beside me *there
> is* no God. And who, as I, shall call, and shall declare it, and set it
> in order for me, since I appointed the ancient people? and the
> things that are coming, and shall come, let them shew unto them.
> Fear ye not, neither be afraid: have not I told thee from that time,
> and have declared *it? ye are* even my witnesses. Is there a God be-
> side me? yea, *there is* no God; I know not *any*. They that make a
> graven image *are* all of them vanity; and their delectable things shall
> not profit; and they *are* their own witnesses; they see not, nor
> know; that they may be ashamed. Who hath formed a god, or mol-
> ten a graven image *that* is profitable for nothing? Behold, all his
> fellows shall be ashamed: and the workmen, they *are* of men: let
> them all be gathered together, let them stand up; *yet* they shall fear,
> *and* they shall be ashamed together. The smith with the tongs both
> worketh in the coals, and fashioneth it with hammers, and worketh
> it with the strength of his arms: yea, he is hungry, and his strength
> faileth; he drinketh no water, and is faint. The carpenter stretcheth
> out *his* rule; he marketh it out with a line; he fitteth it with planes,
> and he marketh it out with the compass, and maketh it after the
> figure of a man, according to the beauty of a man; that it may re-
> main in the house. He heweth him down cedars, and taketh the
> cypress and the oak, which he strengtheneth for himself among
> the trees of the forest: he planteth an ash, and the rain doth nour-
> ish *it*. Then shall it be for a man to burn: for he will take thereof,
> and warm himself; yea, he kindleth *it*, and baketh bread; yea, he
> maketh a god, and worshippeth *it*; he maketh it a graven image,
> and falleth down thereto. He burneth part thereof in the fire; with

part thereof he eateth flesh; he roasteth roast, and is satisfied: yea, he warmeth *himself*, and saith, Aha, I am warm, I have seen the fire: And the residue thereof he maketh a god, *even* his graven image: he falleth down unto it, and worshippeth *it*, and prayeth unto it, and saith, Deliver me; for thou *art* my god. They have not known nor understood: for he hath shut their eyes, that they cannot see; *and* their hearts, that they cannot understand. And none considereth in his heart, neither *is there* knowledge nor understanding to say, I have burned part of it in the fire; yea, also I have baked bread upon the coals thereof; I have roasted flesh, and eaten *it*: and shall I make the residue thereof an abomination? shall I fall down to the stock of a tree? He feedeth on ashes: a deceived heart hath turned him aside, that he cannot deliver his soul, nor say, *Is there* not a lie in my right hand? Isaiah 44:6-20

He proposes to construct the form of God with compass and straightedge; the matter, through wood and precious metals; and the purpose, to warm himself and cook meat. He ought rather to represent the divine nature through obedience to his commandments.[36]

> Behold, I go forward, but he *is* not *there*; and backward, but I cannot perceive him: On the left hand, where he doth work, but I cannot behold *him*; he hideth himself on the right hand, that I cannot see *him*. But he knoweth the way that I take: *when* he hath tried me, I shall come forth as gold. Job 23:8-9

See also Ex. 33:20; Deut. 4:15-19; Jer. 10:1-16; John 1:18; Rom. 1:18-25; Acts 17:22-29; Ex. 25:9, 30:22-38; Ps. 50:7-15; Prov. 21:3; Is. 1:10-20, 29:13, 66:1-3; Jer. 7:21-23; Amos 5:14-27; Mic. 6:6-9; Rom. 12:1; 1 Cor. 7:19.

---

[36] *Worship* is a representation of the divine nature by the rational being. This is done through obedience to God's commandments. *Formal* worship is a mediate representation of the divine nature. All acts of obedience to God are representations of him in the heart of man. *Material* worship is, however, a direct representation of the divine nature, and is therefore limited to those acts of worship that God himself has commanded. The *circumstances* of worship are, nevertheless, still subject to the moral law, and therefore all conditions of worship are governed by the moral law, even when there is no direct command. The acts themselves are, however, to be solely those which God has appointed in his word. *Westminster Confession of Faith* 1.6, 21.1.

Comment

Plurality is the particular thought through unity, whereby the particulars under a given unity are thought of as units mutually excluding one another. Space is an extension,[37] a whole made of parts external to one another, mutually exclusive particulars under a common universal. Whatsoever is represented in space is a plurality.[38] The intuition of the divine nature is identical to its concept, and its concept excludes particularity, which cannot therefore be thought in the divine nature through its unity. There is a negation of plurality in the divine nature that negates all physical representation thereof. God is an inwardly lawful being; any outward representation of his inward lawfulness is intrinsically contradictory.

The attributes of God are particular, as are the duties of the moral law, but, as the Ten Commandments show, particular duties are applications of one law to the visible world. The unity of the law is the lawgiving form[39] applied in each commandment: "Therefore all things whatsoever ye would that men should do to you, do ye even so to them: for this is the law and the prophets" (Matthew 7:12).

The attributes of God are particular, formally the same, materially distinct, distinct relations of one and the same being to different things, as space, time, the world, himself, good men and evil; accordingly, he is omnipresent, eternal, omniscient, unchangeable, benevolent, just, wise.[40]

Unity and plurality combine to form totality,[41] but in God plurality is negative. There is no plurality in the divine nature; therefore, neither is there a divine totality, but a logical totality or conclusion drawn from the first two commandments: "Thou shalt not bow down to them nor worship them…" (Exodus 20:5). Idols are false gods; worship of God through idols is not worship of God, but of idols.

God is invisible; man does not intuit the divine nature. Man knows God, not through an intuition given, but to be produced. The question is not, how is the divine unity intuited in a plurality, but how is it thought in

---

[37] Kant, *Pure Reason*, B202-207.

[38] See footnote 35.

[39] *Groundwork*, 4:416-438; *Practical Reason*, 5:27-28, 5:30-31.

[40] Immanuel Kant, "On the miscarriage of all philosophical trials in theodicy," in *Religion and Rational Theology*, ed. by Allen W. Wood and George di Giovanni, trans. by George di Giovanni (New York: Cambridge University Press, 1996), 8:255-257; *Lectures* 28:1073-76.

[41] *Pure Reason*, B106.

a plurality intuited? Plurality is the mutual exclusion of particulars under a common unity. The divine unity is universality without particularity; particularity without the divine nature, and under it, is in particular thinking subjects, the rational beings whom God has made. These are outwardly lawful beings, made in God's image, free to do good or evil. In the multiplicity of men and the division of their works, the unity of the divine nature is thought, through the happiness or misery of which good and evil men partake.

> Thou shalt not bow down to them nor serve them: for I the LORD thy God *am* a jealous God, visiting the iniquity of the fathers upon the children unto the third and fourth *generation* of them that hate me; And shewing mercy unto thousands of them that love me, and keep my commandments. Exodus 20:5-6

> And the angel of God, which went before the camp of Israel, removed and went behind them; and the pillar of the cloud went from before their face, and stood behind them: And it came between the camp of the Egyptians and the camp of Israel; and it was a cloud and darkness *to them*, but it gave light by night *to these*; so that the one came not near the other all the night. Exodus 14:19-20, cf. 15:19

> And it shall come to pass, that as the LORD rejoiced over you to do you good, and to multiply you; so the LORD will rejoice over you to destroy you, and to bring you to nought; and ye shall be plucked from off the land whither thou goest to possess it. Deuteronomy 28:63

Proposition 3

God has appeared to us in Jesus Christ.

Proof

This proposition may only be known through experience, but its necessity may be demonstrated as follows.

13

The divine unity is thought in a plurality intuited: God rewards the righteous and punishes the wicked, for man either obeys or disobeys the moral law, and God repays every man according to his works. Therefore, the relation of God to man is thought in a disjunction: God justifies or condemns, according as men are good or evil.

Salvation is the transition from condemnation to justification, and a moment of transition combines before and after.[42] Accordingly, neither condemnation nor justification alone suffices to save men from their sins. Sinners ought not to be justified, nor righteous men condemned. By logical division of God's works there is no possibility of salvation.

The whole of God's judgments is possible in another way, through their community and reciprocity.[43] If salvation is not possible through the former, we may appeal to the latter. A disjunctive judgment contains the mutual exclusion of particulars under a common universal; community and reciprocity contain the mutual determination of the plurality of intuition within its unity. The plurality of judgments consists of justification and condemnation; their community and reciprocity is their union in one man, Jesus Christ; and this union is possible through the unity of the divine nature exhibited therein. Therefore, Jesus Christ reveals the divine nature through the harmony of diverse judgments executed upon himself.

Scripture Proof

> For Christ also hath once suffered for sins, the just for the unjust, that he might bring us to God, being put to death in the flesh, but quickened by the Spirit. 1 Peter 3:18

Christ suffered to save us, *to bring us to God*, by revealing God to us, *being put to death in the flesh, but quickened by the Spirit.*

> And without controversy great is the mystery of godliness: God was manifest in the flesh, justified in the Spirit. 1 Timothy 3:16

Justified in the Spirit, justified in his submission to the condemnation of the Father, and rewarded with the divine name.

---

[42] Aristotle, *Metaphysics* 217b29-222b29.
[43] Kant, *Pure Reason*, B111-113.

14

Who, being in the form of God, thought it not robbery to be equal with God: But made himself of no reputation, and took upon him the form of a servant, and was made in the likeness of men: And being found in fashion as a man, he humbled himself, and became obedient unto death, even the death of the cross. Wherefore God also hath highly exalted him, and given him a name which is above every name: That at the name of Jesus every knee should bow, of *things* in heaven, and *things* in earth, and *things* under the earth; And *that* every tongue should confess that Jesus Christ *is* Lord, to the glory of God the Father. Philippians 2:6-11

Through justification of his obedience under the sentence of condemnation, the divine nature appears to men in human form.

The law divides between right and wrong, life and death.

See, I have set before thee this day life and good, and death and evil; In that I command thee this day to love the LORD thy God, to walk in his ways, and to keep his commandments and his statutes and his judgments, that thou mayest live and multiply: and the LORD thy God shall bless thee in the land whither thou goest to possess it. But if thine heart turn away, so that thou wilt not hear, but shalt be drawn away, and worship other gods, and serve them; I denounce unto you this day, that ye shall surely perish, *and that* ye shall not prolong *your* days upon the land, whither thou passest over Jordan to go to possess it. I call heaven and earth to record this day against you, *that* I have set before you life and death, blessing and cursing: therefore choose life, that both thou and thy seed may live: That thou mayest love the LORD thy God, *and* that thou mayest obey his voice, and that thou mayest cleave unto him: for he *is* thy life, and the length of thy days: that thou mayest dwell in the land which the LORD sware unto thy fathers, to Abraham, to Isaac, and to Jacob, to give them. Deuteronomy 30:15-20, cf. chapters 27-30

The moral law suffices to condemn man. The law of Moses was not given to man to condemn him, long before the day of judgment, to fan the flames of his sin, to muddy his wallows, for he says,

> Say unto them, *As* I live, saith the Lord GOD, I have no pleasure in the death of the wicked; but that the wicked turn from his way and live: turn ye, turn ye from your evil ways; for why will ye die, O house of Israel? Ezekiel 33:11, cf. Rom. 7:1-13

If God speaks to condemn, he condemns; and if he does not condemn, then he speaks not to condemn, but to save.

> But his wife said unto him, If the LORD were pleased to kill us, he would not have received a burnt offering and a meat offering at our hands, neither would he have shewed us all these *things*, nor would as at this time have told us *such things* as these. Judges 13:23

> For God sent not his Son into the world to condemn the world; but that the world through him might be saved. John 3:17

> Or despisest thou the riches of his goodness and forbearance and longsuffering; not knowing that the goodness of God leadeth thee to repentance? Romans 2:4

What the letter of the law divides, the spirit of the law harmonizes; through the spoken word of God the opposition is transformed into agreement.

> For the law was given through Moses, *but* grace and truth came by Jesus Christ. John 1:17

Grace distinct from truth, working together with it. Grace to condemn our sins in Christ; truth to justify Christ in bearing our sins. Grace and truth together to show the Father in the Son.

> And the Word was made flesh, and dwelt among us, (and we beheld his glory, glory as of the only begotten of the Father,) full of grace and truth. John 1:14

> And the LORD descended in the cloud, and stood with him there, and proclaimed the name of the LORD. And the LORD passed by before him, and proclaimed, The LORD, the LORD God, merciful

and gracious, longsuffering, and abundant in goodness and truth, Keeping mercy for thousands, forgiving iniquity and transgression and sin, and that will by no means clear *the guilty*; visiting the iniquity of the fathers upon the children, and upon the children's children, unto the third and to the fourth *generation*. Exodus 34:5-7, cf. 33:12-34:7.

Here opposites are joined: *forgiving iniquity and transgression and sin, and that will by no means clear the guilty*. The elect, once forgiven, are no more guilty— then they are cleared, for God requires it of Christ, and in him, of us. It is Christ, who *descended in the cloud, and stood with him there, and proclaimed the name of the LORD*, who *passed by before him*, and proclaimed that God forgives sin without clearing the guilty.

Surely his salvation *is* nigh them that fear him; that glory may dwell in our land. Mercy and truth are met together; righteousness and peace have kissed *each other*. Ps. 85:9-10

Comment

Unity and plurality are identified in totality. They are distinct in thought, identical in intuition. Given a plurality and its unity, the totality follows—for example, a determinate quantity—because their synthesis is an act of the thinking subject.[44] If either is not given, then neither is the totality; or if the totality is given instead, the remaining term is given through the other two, as the remaining part of a whole whose parts are given. If, then, either a unity or plurality is given, one without the other, the totality is an idea, a concept without an intuition,[45] for if there is a concept of each, and only one is given, the totality is conceived, but not intuited.

The unity of space is thought; the plurality of particular spaces, intuited. Space is therefore finite or infinite; either the unity of space is itself a particular space, or the plurality of space is itself the universal space.[46] Both are false, neither is complete.[47] The progress alone is given to us, from one

---

[44] Kant, *Pure Reason*, B110-111, B129-130.
[45] *Pure Reason*, B368-377. This is Kant's definition of "idea."
[46] *Pure Reason*, B513-518.
[47] *Pure Reason*, B530-535.

space to another;[48] the completeness is an idea, formed from the identification of a concept and its intuition. The totality of space is therefore only the idea of a whole in a disjunctive judgment, in which neither member is true, because the concept of space is common to both its unity and its plurality, and a logical totality is a disjunctive judgment, but the intuition required for a determination to either disjunct is lacking.[49]

Thus, the totality of the divine nature might perhaps comprise an intuition given, or at least a concept without an intuition, that is, an idea, but because the divine plurality is a negation thereof, a totality is not only not given, but inconceivable, and its concept is empty. All theoretical arguments for God's existence prove his non-existence to boot; such arguments assume the divine totality, a concept not in consciousness, which may therefore be freely affirmed or denied.[50] God is, in himself, unknowable to man; the Lord is known through his works.[51]

If man perseveres in obedience to the moral law, then the logical division of God's work suffices for man's happiness; but if he sins, then the knowledge of God in man requires that he be punished, and gives no hope of salvation. Man in his innocence is free to fall, because to negate the law as a universal, he need only depart from it in one instance; but having fallen, he is unable of himself to repent, because the law requires all his actions to be in agreement with it; he has made the law no more universal and necessary, but himself a transgressor of it.[52]

---

[48] Kant, *Pure Reason*, B536-543.

[49] Cf. Matt. 8:12, 22:13, 25:30; Ps. 37:10.

[50] *Pure Reason*, B694-696, B723-730.

Anselm's Ontological Argument: God is that than which nothing greater can be conceived, but something greater than God can be conceived, namely, that which is greater than that than which nothing greater can be conceived. Therefore, God does not exist. Anselm, *Proslogion* Chapters 2-4.

Aquinas' Cosmological Argument: Every alteration is caused, so the chain of causes and effects is regressively infinite. Therefore, there is no first cause, and because God is the first cause, there is no God. Aquinas, *Summa* 1.2.3.

Physico-Theological Argument: Everything that works towards an end is impelled by a mind, but the ends of nature are finite; therefore, there is no infinite mind impelling things toward their ends. Thus, God does not exist. *Summa* 1.2.3.

[51] Ex. 6:6-8, 7:3-5, 14:4, 18; Ps. 9:16; Is. 19:21; Ezek. 28:22, 30:26.

[52] 1 Kings 21:25; Jer. 13:23; John 8:34; Romans 6:16; Jas. 2:10-11; Kant, *Religion*, 6:24-25. Kant argues that the possibility of repentance is as incomprehensible as that of the fall, and therefore we may be excused from the former, as we are from the latter (Kant, *Religion*, 6:50-51). However, I regard an explanation of both as necessary, for if indeed man were able to convert himself, he would also understand the ground of this possibility.

Salvation is possible through knowledge of God other than that of his nature, through that of his persons, who are known not through the concept of God, but through intuition. The divine unity, being invisible, must therefore be intuited, indirectly, in a totality, and this totality depends upon a visible plurality, which is thought through the divine unity, and is itself a unity, and is not divine, but human. This is the plurality of judgments executed upon one man, Jesus Christ.

Man is an outwardly lawful being of sensible intuition, under the moral law, free to do good or evil, of a visible body, a plurality of parts; man's happiness, distinct from his lawfulness, is in the objects of sense, which have their pleasurable effect on man's animal nature. Man is visible, his legal state is an appearance, and the plurality of judgments is manifested in Christ, blessed misery bespeaking divine fullness.

Thus, having demonstrated the possibility of the fall from innocence, I also seek to explain the possibility of repentance in the Gospel. I agree with Kant, that what is commanded must be presupposed possible, but only for the sake of practical purposes, and therefore Kant's argument begs the question, for because man is lost in sin, he has no insight into the possibility of repentance, until he hears the Gospel. See *Religion*, 6:44-45.

PART I—THE INCARNATION

SECTION 2—THE IMAGE OF GOD

Definition

The moral quality of a person is the matter of the law, whether good or evil; his relation to the law, or legal state, is innocence or guilt.

Explication

> The LORD shall judge the people: judge me, O LORD, according to my righteousness, and according to mine integrity that is in me. Psalm 7:8

> The LORD hath recompensed me according to my righteousness, according to the cleanness of my hands in his eyesight. Psalm 18:20

> Judge me, O LORD; for I have walked in mine integrity: I have trusted also in the LORD; *therefore* I shall not slide. Examine me, O LORD, and prove me; try my reins and my heart. Psalm 27:1-2, see also Lev. 1:4, 4:13, 22, 31, 35, 5:1-6, 10, 13, 17-19, 6:4, 7:18, 10:17 &etc., 2 Ch. 6:23.

He is righteous, and the Lord judges him to be so. These are therefore distinguished, being different relations of the same law to different things, whether to the object, or to the subject. The law prescribes an intuition to be produced, and an intuition is the thought of a non-thought. The non-thought element is the moral quality or character of the person; the thought element is his legal state. The former pertains to the person judged; the latter to the person judging.

A moral judgment is the subjective representation of the character of a person. This judgment ought to agree with the moral quality of the person. Though man may err in judgment, God does not err; in him, sin and guilt, righteousness and innocence, reciprocally imply one another. God's judgment of a man is his legal state, and the rule of our judgment: "Keep thee far from a false matter; and the innocent and righteous slay thou not: for I will not justify the wicked" (Exodus 23:7).

There is no other legal state besides innocence and guilt; yet there is a legal state besides them, which is not a legal state, nonlegal righteousness, which belongs to God. God is an inwardly lawful being. He is not bound by the law, nor judged by it, for he himself is the lawgiver and judge, who binds men and angels to the law, and judges them according to their works. He is not under the law, but above it, a singularly lawful being, in whom the law is particular, and he, the being of the law.[1]

Nonlegal righteousness is a negation of the law that itself affirms it. God is righteous without law.[2] His righteousness is not by the law, nor can it be understood by the law, neither without it. It is outside the law, and therefore outside of any sensible intuition given in accordance with the law.

> For my thoughts *are* not your thoughts, neither *are* your ways my ways, saith the LORD. For *as* the heavens are higher than the earth, so are my ways higher than your ways, and my thoughts than your thoughts. Isaiah 55:8-9

"And when the children of Israel saw *it*, they said one to another, It *is* manna: for they wist not what it *was*," but that which we know not, is known by this quality of not being known (Exodus 16:14-15). The angel said to Jacob, "Wherefore *is* it *that* thou dost ask after my name?" (Genesis 32:29). It is a question and a problem; "manna," *what is it?* It is a secret. "Why askest thou thus after my name, seeing it *is* secret?" (Judges 13:18); "And he had a name written, that no man knew, but he himself" (Revelation 19:12).

Proposition 1

Jesus Christ is innocent.

---

[1] Kant, *Lectures*, 28:1076.
[2] Rom. 3:11; 1 Tim. 1:8-11.

Proof

God reveals himself through the human nature of Jesus Christ. God is nonlegally righteous; if man knows God, then not otherwise. This legal state cannot be given directly to man; therefore indirectly, through another in agreement with it, and before the law as Christ is man. A legal state that agrees with nonlegal righteousness is one of righteousness, which before the law is innocence. Therefore, Jesus Christ is innocent.

Scripture Proof

> But when the fullness of the time was come, God sent forth his Son, made of a woman, made under the law, To redeem them that were under the law, that we might receive the adoption of sons. Galatians 4:4-5

If righteous, and under the law, then righteous under the law, righteousness revealing righteousness.

> Who, being in the form of God, thought it not robbery to be equal with God: But made himself of no reputation, and took upon him the form of a servant, and was made in the likeness of men: And being found in fashion as a man, he humbled himself, and became obedient unto death, even the death of the cross. Wherefore God also hath highly exalted him, and given him a name which is above every name: That at the name of Jesus every knee should bow, of *things* in heaven, and *things* in earth, and *things* under the earth; And *that* every tongue should confess that Jesus Christ *is* Lord, to the glory of God the Father. Philippians 2:6-11

Obedient to the law, therefore justified by the law; justified by the law, therefore rewarded by the law. And what is his reward? A name above every name, the divine name, and a name makes known the one named. Therefore, by the law Christ shows himself above the law.

> Behold my servant, whom I uphold; mine elect, *in whom* my soul delighteth; I have put my spirit upon him: he shall bring forth judgment to the Gentiles. He shall not cry, nor lift up, nor cause his

23

voice to be heard in the street. A bruised reed shall he not break, and the smoking flax shall he not quench: he shall bring forth judgment unto truth. He shall not fail nor be discouraged, till he have set judgment in the earth: and the isles shall wait for his law. Thus saith God the LORD, he that created the heavens, and stretched them out; he that spread forth the earth, and that which cometh out of it; he that giveth breath unto the people upon it, and spirit to them that walk therein: I the LORD have called thee in righteousness, and will hold thine hand, and will keep thee, and give thee for a covenant of the people, for a light of the Gentiles; To open the blind eyes, to bring out the prisoners from the prison, *and* them that sit in darkness out of the prison house. I *am* the LORD: that *is* my name: and my glory will I not give to another, neither my praise to graven images. Isaiah 42:1-8, cf. vs. 19-21

He who is God's servant, and performs works divine, himself is God, for God says, *my glory will I not give to another, neither my praise to graven images.* He is righteous, and he is more than righteous, for God upholds him, and has put his spirit upon him, *and he shall bring forth judgment to the Gentiles,* for the law is his, *and the isles shall wait for his law,* for he is the lawgiver. Divinity is added to his servitude, servitude to his divinity; in Christ, there is not one without the other. His righteousness is one, as under the law, as above it, accomplishing divine works through human nature.

See also 1 John 2:1; Matt. 3:15-17; Rom. 5:18-21; Rom. 8:3-4; Heb. 2:10-17.

Comment

The quantity of concepts thinks the particular through the universal. *Through* refers to the relation of universal to particular. The quality of concepts thinks the universal through the particular, as the particular is thought through the universal. Therefore, quality is itself thought through quantity, and both together think the universal through itself. These are the constitutive principles of concepts, and of intuitions thought through concepts.[3]

---

[3] Kant, *Pure Reason*, B110, B199-200, B220-223.

The universal form of the quality of concepts is affirmation. Affirmation affirms the universal of the particular, thinking the universal through the particular, as that to which the universal applies. The particular form of the quality of concepts is negation. Negation denies one particular of another, thinking the universal in the particular, as that which is common to the others.

The forms of quality are affirmation and negation.[4] This is the intension of concepts.[5] What is affirmed of a thing is affirmed of it, as a universal of a particular. What is denied of a thing is denied of it, as one particular of another under a common universal.

If the particular lies outside the concept of the universal, under another, the judgment is infinite.[6] An infinite judgment identifies affirmation and negation.[7] Affirmation and negation are distinct in thought, identical in intuition. Thus, whereas intuition was defined before as a representation of all that is thought under a concept as within the concept itself, it is now defined also as the thought of that which is other than thought, the thought of a non-thought.

Intuition is therefore a thought, and is thought through the logical forms of judgment; as to quality, through affirmation and negation, whether as thought or non-thought. As thought, an intuition's affirmation is the plurality thought within its unity, and refers to the simplicity of an object. Negation is the mutual exclusion of its parts, and refers to the object's complexity.

Sensible objects appear to be either simple or complex. Every complex object is made of parts, either simple or complex, and there is either a finite progression to parts simple, or an infinite progression to parts complex.[8] Neither of these is true. An object of experience is not given in its parts, but in its progression to the parts.[9] Experience gives the relations of a thing, not the thing in itself.[10]

---

[4] Kant, *Pure Reason*, B95, B97-98.
[5] *Pure Reason*, B96-97; *Logic*, Sections 7-16, 21-22; Reich, *Completeness*, 31-39. Quantity refers to the extension of concepts.
[6] Kant, *Pure Reason*, B97-98; *Logic*, Section 22.
[7] *Pure Reason*, B97-98; *Logic*, Section 22.
[8] *Pure Reason*, B463-471. Kant's second antinomy.
[9] *Pure Reason*, B536-545, B551-555.
[10] *Pure Reason*, B504-535.

This antinomy arises from the identification of appearances and things in themselves, for if concepts and intuitions are identified, then the intuitions are given in logical connection with one another; but if distinguished, then the intuitions are given only through an intuitive connection, that is, the actual breaking of substances into their components.

As non-thought, an intuition's affirmation is the plurality intuited within its unity, and refers to its reality. The intuition's negation is the cohesion of its parts, and refers to its degree. Sensations are intensive magnitudes. Whereas extensive magnitudes represent the whole through its parts, intensive magnitudes represent the parts through the whole. Intensive magnitudes do not distinguish their parts from one another, but only from the whole, in the sensation's degree. All that is seen in a ray of light is seen in a single glance, but may be increased, or diminished to nothing.

God's reality is invisibility within unity; God's invisibility is a negation of plurality. God is therefore simple.[11] Affirmation of negation is infinity; therefore, the being of God is infinite,[12] and surpasses all others. He is the most real being, the supreme being, the being of all beings,[13] and possesses a name above every other, never to be used as a means at all, but only as an end, as the supreme end of all things.

> Thou shalt not take the name of the LORD thy God in vain, for the LORD will not hold him guiltless that taketh his name in vain. Exodus 20:7

There is no plurality in God's being, but there is plurality in the visible works of God, in natural purposes, the symbols of moral purposes, and of the divine unity. These exclude one another as parts of a whole, and are divided into six days of work, and a seventh of rest.

> Remember the sabbath day, to keep it holy. Six days shalt thou labor, and do all thy work: but the seventh day *is* the sabbath of the LORD thy God: *in it* thou shalt not do any work, thou, nor thy son, nor thy daughter, thy manservant, nor thy maidservant, nor thy cattle, nor thy stranger that *is* within thy gates: For *in* six days

---

[11] Kant, *Pure Reason*, B599-608; Aquinas, *Summa* 1.3.
[12] Kant, *Pure Reason*, B604; Aquinas, *Summa* 1.7.1.
[13] Kant, *Pure Reason*, B606-607; Aquinas, *Summa* 1.4.2-3, 1.6.2-3, 1.44.1.

the LORD made heaven and earth, the sea, and all that in them *is*, and rested the seventh day: wherefore the LORD blessed the sabbath day, and hallowed it. Exodus 20:8-11

The divine nature revealed in the flesh and blood of Jesus Christ is a totality—the unity of the divine nature in a plurality of divine judgments. The reality of this revelation is the plurality of judgments within the unity of the divine nature. A particular agrees with its universal, a plurality with its unity. Therefore, Christ's legal state agrees with the divine nature, and is a representation of one and the same righteousness, as under the law, as above it. This legal state is innocence.

Innocence is the necessary condition of the fleshly manifestation of the divine nature. If Christ is God, then he is righteous; if not righteous, then not God; but it does not follow that if he is righteous under the law, then he is God, for something more than righteousness is thought in non-legal righteousness. Nevertheless, negation is thought through affirmation,[14] the mutual exclusion of particulars through the common universal, and therefore, without legal affirmation, there is no legal negation, and without these, there is no intuition of the divine nature.

Proposition 2

Jesus Christ was condemned.

Proof

Christ is righteous before the law. The concept of the divine nature contains, besides the affirmation of God's righteousness, a negation of the law, as that standard by which he is to be judged. Under the law, Christ agrees with the divine affirmation, to show forth the divine nature, therefore also with the divine negation. This negation, as man, is a negation of Christ's legal standing before God, which is condemnation. Therefore, to show forth the divine nature, Jesus Christ was condemned.

---

[14] Kant, *Pure Reason*, B603.

Scripture Proof

> Who, being in the form of God, thought it not robbery to be equal with God: But made himself of no reputation, and took upon him the form of a servant, and was made in the likeness of men: And being found in fashion as a man, he humbled himself, and became obedient unto death, even the death of the cross. Wherefore God also hath highly exalted him, and given him a name which is above every name, That at the name of Jesus every knee might bow, of *things* in heaven, and *things* in earth, and *things* under the earth; And *that* every tongue should confess, that Jesus Christ *is* Lord. Philippians 2:6-11

Obedience deserves reward; obedience under condemnation is divine, and deserves divine reward.

> For Christ also hath once suffered for sins, the just for the unjust, that he might bring us to God, being put to death in the flesh, but quickened by the spirit. 1 Peter 3:18

The Spirit justifying, and Christ saving, are God. Christ brings us to God, by bringing God to us: righteous, though condemned, he shows us the Father.

> For he hath made him *to be* sin for us, who knew no sin; that we might be made the righteousness of God in him. 2 Corinthians 5:21

He is the righteousness of God, and we in him. And the righteousness of God is this, that he who knew no sin, be made sin for us.

> Surely he hath borne our griefs, and carried our sorrows: yet we did esteem him stricken, smitten of God, and afflicted. But he *was* wounded for our transgressions, *he was* bruised for our iniquities: the chastisement of our peace *was* upon him; and with his stripes we are healed. All we like sheep have gone astray; we have turned every one to his own way; and the LORD hath laid on him the iniquity of us all. He was oppressed, and he was afflicted, yet he

opened not his mouth: he is brought as a lamb to the slaughter, and as a sheep before her shearers is dumb, so he openeth not his mouth. He was taken from prison and from judgment: and who shall declare his generation? For he was cut off out of the land of the living: for the transgression of my people was he stricken. And he made his grave with the wicked, and with the rich in his death; because he had done no violence, neither *was any* deceit in his mouth. Yet it pleased the LORD to bruise him; he hath put *him* to grief: when thou shalt make his soul an offering for sin, he shall see *his* seed, he shall prolong *his* days, and the pleasure of the LORD shall prosper in his hand. He shall see of the travail of his soul, *and* shall be satisfied: by his knowledge shall my righteous servant justify many; for he shall bear their iniquities. Therefore will I divide him *a portion* with the great, and he shall divide the spoil with the strong; because he hath poured out his soul unto death: and he was numbered with the transgressors; and he bare the sin of many, and made intercession for the transgressors. Isaiah 53:4-12

It was the Father's pleasure to bruise him, to condemn him for our sins, that he should merit our salvation, and show us the love of God.

Comment

One particular is distinguished from another under a common universal through *negation*. Negation distinguishes the plurality of an intuition through the representation of a common unity. When that unity precedes the plurality, the parts exclude one another by measure.[15] When the plurality precedes the unity, the parts include one another by degree.[16] Both extensive and intensive magnitudes subsist through negation, whereby the plurality of parts represents the unity of the whole, greater or less.

The unity of the divine nature is intuited in the plurality of judgments executed upon Christ. The necessary condition of this totality is the unity of the divine nature in the judgments executed. The particular judgments agree in the revelation of divine righteousness. Agreement with the divine righteousness is itself righteous. Therefore, the necessary condition of the

---

[15] Kant, *Pure Reason*, B203-204.
[16] *Pure Reason*, B207-211.

manifestation of the divine nature is that Christ is judged righteous, or, that he is innocent.

The unity of the judgments is Christ's innocence. Plurality of judgment requires another to oppose Christ's innocence in agreement with the divine nature, to unite these judgments in a totality. The judgment that opposes justification is condemnation: Christ is righteous under condemnation, and is justified therein. The quality of his righteousness, as above the law, is revealed through condemnation. The plurality of judgments is a representation of one and the same righteousness, as under the law, as under condemnation, and the plurality of judgments executed upon Christ represents the divine unity.

Christ's condemnation is the sufficient condition of the revelation of the divine nature; by it the judgments executed upon Christ form a plurality through their opposition. If Christ is righteous under condemnation, then he is also nonlegally righteous, but this condemnation is not yet that divine righteousness. To show forth the unity of the divine nature, the plurality of judgments must form a totality.

The nerve of the proof is, that God and fallen man have something in common, and that divinity can be represented through the form of sinful humanity, without the matter, for sin represents righteousness formally through its absence, as darkness light. "God sending his own Son in the likeness of sinful flesh, and for sin, condemned sin in the flesh" (Romans 8:1-4, cf. 2 Cor. 5:21). Sin is a formal representation of the divine nature, for it strives to be like God, to partake of a nonlegal righteousness, yet it falls short, "for all have sinned, and come short of the glory of God" (Romans 3:23).[17] The sinner thinks himself to be as God, above the law; but in God, negation of the law is itself an affirmation of his righteousness; in sinners, it is negation of the law, and of righteousness.[18] Therefore, when a man sees Christ condemned, and his submission to condemnation, he may understand that Christ's righteousness resides outside the sphere of the law, in the divine nature.

Proposition 3

Jesus Christ is nonlegally righteous as God.

---

[17] Gen. 3:5, 22; Is. 14:12-14, 47:10; Ez. 28:1-19.
[18] Ps. 21:11.

Proof

Jesus Christ is righteous under condemnation, and that condemnation is itself a representation of his righteousness, because every legal state forms a representation of the moral quality of the person. However, Christ's condemnation cannot represent his righteousness, only his innocence; therefore, that condemnation must be taken together with his innocence, and these are combined in nonlegal righteousness. Christ's righteousness is therefore not only under the law, but also above it, and he himself is God, being nonlegally righteous.

Scripture Proof

> Who, being in the form of God, thought it not robbery to be equal with God: But made himself of no reputation, and took upon him the form of a servant, and was made in the likeness of men: And being found in fashion as a man, he humbled himself, and became obedient unto death, even the death of the cross. Wherefore God also hath highly exalted him, and given him a name which is above every name: That at the name of Jesus every knee should bow, of *things* in heaven, and *things* in earth, and *things* under the earth; And *that* every tongue should confess that Jesus Christ *is* Lord, to the glory of God the Father. Philippians 2:6-11

> For Christ also hath once suffered for sins, the just for the unjust, that he might bring us to God, being put to death in the flesh, but quickened by the spirit. 1 Peter 3:18

> Awake, O sword, against my shepherd, and against the man *that is* my fellow, saith the LORD of hosts: smite the shepherd, and the sheep shall be scattered: and I will turn mine hand upon the little ones. Zechariah 13:7

The savior shows himself, a man, to be God, through his obedience under the condemnation of the Father, for salvation is the work of God.

> If I ascend up into heaven, thou *art* there: if I make my bed in hell, behold, thou *art there*. *If* I take the wings of the morning, *and* dwell

31

in the uttermost parts of the sea; Even there shall thy hand lead me, and thy right hand shall hold me. If I say, surely the darkness shall cover me; even the night shall be light about me. Yea, the darkness hideth not from thee; but the night shineth as the day: the darkness and the light *are* both alike *to thee*. For thou hast possessed my reins: thou hast covered me in my mother's womb. Psalm 139:8-12

The world was made in darkness; out of darkness, light. God condemns Christ, and out of his condemnation, justification comes, for they are both alike to God, and together they reveal him to us.

Comment

An infinite judgment negates the universal of the particular.[19] Because there is no particular that does not stand under some universal, the particular of an infinite judgment stands under another universal, opposed to the former universal, as one particular to another, which both therefore stand under a universal higher than either.

The form of infinite judgment applies to intuition in the category of limitation.[20] Affirmation thinks the plurality of intuition within its unity; negation thinks the parts of the plurality distinguished from one another; limitation thinks the boundary of intuition, and the plurality outside the unity of intuition. Sensation is finite; for every degree of sensation there is a lesser, and a greater.[21]

The sensation of a space is affirmed within its boundary, negated without. As the perception of space, so of time. Past time is perceived within the present; future time is excluded; the present is its boundary.

The objects of experience are affirmed within the form of experience; bounded by transcendental principles, they exclude objects of intellectual intuition, and limit our experience to the objects of sense.[22]

The divine unity revealed in the plurality of judgments executed upon Christ forms a totality, and the particular legal states of Christ form a single legal state. Opposites agree with one another through mutual agreement

---

[19] Kant, *Pure Reason*, B97-98; *Logic*, Section 22.
[20] *Pure Reason*, B106.
[21] *Pure Reason*, B209-218.
[22] *Pure Reason*, B266-267, B310-311.

with their combination. The synthesis of an affirmation and a negation is an infinite judgment, and the synthesis of justification and condemnation is nonlegal righteousness. This legal state belongs, as the prior states, to Christ's person.[23] Therefore, the nature represented in this legal state is also predicated of Christ. The former states belong to Christ as man; the latter belongs to him as God. Jesus Christ is therefore both man and God.

The doctrine of the totality of divine judgments teaches that Christ reveals the divine nature to us through the harmony of diverse judgments executed upon him. The doctrine of the limitation of Christ's legal states teaches us that Christ himself is God, and that he reveals the divine nature to us because he himself possesses it. That he possesses the divine nature, is proven from the revelation he makes of it, because the divine nature is revealed by its legal state, and its legal state is revealed by the justification and condemnation of Christ, and these belong to Christ, therefore also nonlegal righteousness, and the divine nature.

Appearances are symbols of things in themselves, and are lawful to produce an intuition of things in themselves.[24] In Christ, diverse judgments are harmonized in the divine nature revealed. Christ therefore lawfully takes the human nature to the divine, to show forth the divine.

The nonlegal righteousness of God is intuited in Christ, but there is no further explication of it through the categories, because it is given indirectly through the harmony of opposing legal states. Man does not thereby acquire any theoretical insight[25] into the divine nature, but only practical[26] knowledge for the possibility of salvation.

> The secret *things belong* unto the LORD our God, but those *things which are* revealed *belong* unto us and to our children, that *we* may do all the words of this law. Deuteronomy 29:29

---

[23] Aristotle, *Metaphysics* IV.2, X; Kant, *Pure Reason*, B95-113. Opposites belong to the same class, therefore also their combination.

[24] *Judgment*, ak. 195-198, 240, 298-303, 341, 344-346, 351-355, 246'-247'; Julian Gress, *The Harmony of Reason and the Possibility of Man's Final End in Kant's Critique of Judgment*, revised (juliangress.mywriting.network: Julian Gress, 2018), 35-41.

[25] Kant, *Pure Reason*, Bxxix-xxxi, B817-819.

[26] *Pure Reason*, Bxxix-xxxiii, B845-846, B848-859; *Practical Reason*, 5:132-146, *Judgment*, ak. 453-459.

For God, who commanded the light to shine out of darkness, hath shined in our hearts, to *give* the light of the knowledge of the glory of God in the face of Jesus Christ. 2 Corinthians 4:6

For this cause I bow my knees unto the Father of our Lord Jesus Christ, Of whom the whole family in heaven and earth is named, That he would grant you, according to the riches of his glory, to be strengthened with might by his Spirit in the inner man; That Christ may dwell in your hearts by faith; that ye, being rooted and grounded in love, May be able to comprehend with all saints what *is* the breadth, and length, and depth, and height; And to know the love of Christ, which passeth knowledge, that ye might be filled with all the fullness of God. Ephesians 3:14-19

PART II—THE TRINITY

SECTION 3—THE PERSONS OF GOD

Definition

A person is a moral subject, that which is good or evil.[1]

Explication

A divine person is a divine subject: "In the beginning God created the heaven and the earth" (Genesis 1:1). The predicate, "created," *bara*, is singular, but the subject, "God," *Elohim*, is plural. The divine nature is one, the persons are three. The divine nature is rational and moral; therefore, a person in general is the subject of a rational nature, or a moral subject.

The three persons are then named: "And the Spirit of God moved upon the face of the waters. And God said..." (Genesis 1:2-3). The divine nature is invisible, but the persons appear: God, the Word, and the Spirit of God.

"In the beginning was the Word, and the Word was with God, and the Word was God" (John 1:1). *The Word,* the subject, is God *with God,* a distinct person.

> God... Hath in these last days spoken unto us by *his* Son, whom he hath appointed heir of all things, by whom also he made the worlds; Who being the brightness of *his* glory, and the express image of his person, and upholding all things by the word of his power, when he had by himself purged our sins, sat down on the right hand of the Majesty on high. Hebrews 1:1-3

All of which are predicates of the divine subject, υποστασις, that which stands under the divine nature.

> Holy, holy, holy, *is* the LORD of hosts: the whole earth *is* full of his glory. Isaiah 6:3

---

[1] Kant, *Practical Reason*, 5:66.

Holiness is predicated three times of God, because of three divine subjects.[2]

The thinking subject is the unconditioned condition of thought;[3] thought is predicated of the thinking subject, but the thinking subject is not predicated of anything else in turn.[4] Rather, the thinking subject conceives of an object, as that which is universal to thought, to which thought is particular. In thought, therefore, the universal and the particular are identified. This union is the singular, the form of the intuition of an object.

The moral law is, however, a concept that contains the ground of an intuition. Therefore, the particular concept of the moral law is the thinking subject, which is the ground of the concept of an object, and therefore also of an intuition in agreement with the concept of an object. The law prescribes an intuition of the thinking subject, who is an end in itself, a person.[5]

An intuition produced may either agree or disagree with the moral law, and a person is either good or evil, for a person is an absolute unity.[6] A person ought therefore to be judged and repaid according to his works. Because judgment belongs to God alone, a divine person is one who judges, who rewards or punishes for his own sake, and whose manifestation in judgment is a supreme end of the law.

The divine nature is an absolute unity, and cannot by itself distinguish the persons, because it belongs to each one in common.[7] The persons must therefore be distinguished by the relation of each to the divine nature, and to one another. The divine nature is a pure unity, and there are three and only three pure a priori relations: independence, dependence, and interdependence;[8] besides them there are none, for interdependence combines the

---

[2] Augustine, *The Trinity* 5.2.9.

[3] Kant, *Pure Reason*, B131-139, B377-432, A348-405.

[4] *Pure Reason*, A348-351, A404, B407, B410-413.

[5] Ex. 20:12-17; Lev. 19:18; Matt. 5:13-16, 7:12, 22:39; Mark 12:31; Jas. 1:22-25; *Groundwork*, 4:428-431; *Practical Reason*, 5:86-89; Immanuel Kant, *Metaphysics of Morals*, ed. by Mary Gregor, trans. by Mary Gregor (Cambridge: Cambridge University Press, 1996), 6:223, 434-435, 442. For example, lying is always wrong, because it is a false representation of one's inner state.

[6] *Metaphysics of Morals*, 6:278; *Pure Reason*, A361-366, B407-408.

[7] Aquinas, *Summa* 40.2; *Westminster Larger Catechism* Q.9.A.

[8] Kant, *Pure Reason*, B106; *Logic*, Sections 23-29.

former, which are opposites, and it is the nature of opposites to oppose any other member of the sphere that they occupy.[9]

There are, then, three and only three divine persons, distinguished by the aforesaid relations: the Father, the Son, and the Holy Spirit; besides them there are none. The Father possesses the divine nature independently, the Son dependently on the Father, and the Spirit dependently on both the Father and the Son, who depend upon one another in his procession.[10]

The divine nature belongs to all the persons in common, and whatsoever is proper to the nature, such as the attributes of God, and his works. To each divine person belongs a unique role, according to his peculiar relation, and whatsoever pertains to the relation of each.

The persons are three, and what belongs to them; but the divine nature, and every property of it, is one. The person of Christ is one, and whatsoever belongs to his person, but the nature of Christ, and everything that pertains to his nature, is two.[11]

The moral quality of a man, who by nature is free to do good or evil, is proper to his nature, but the legal state of a man is the relation of the law to his person, and belongs to his person.

The law of God requires that the righteous be justified and the wicked condemned; the law requires agreement between a man's legal state and his moral quality, that the one should represent the other. How then is it possible for God to condemn a righteous man?

The lawfulness of a legal state is the intuition it produces of a person. One person may represent another through its relation to the other, and therefore the person manifested may be the same as the one judged, or different. If the same, a man's legal state is lawful through the intuition it produces of his works. If different, the legal state of the one is lawful through the intuition it produces of the other, as the one person represents the other, because this itself is an intuition of both the representer and the represented.

All legal states are judgments of the lawgiver, and are lawful through a holy judge. A legal state is the relation of a person to the law and is lawful through the law itself represented therein. The relation of the law to a person depends upon the being of the law itself, because obedience to the law

---

[9] Gen. 2:18-25; Ex. 20:12-14; 1 Cor. 7:1-5; 11:1-12; Reich, *Completeness*, 103-109.

[10] John 13:31-17:26; Rom. 8:9-11; Gal. 4:6.

[11] "For my Father is greater than I" (John 14:28). Not greater in nature, but in person. Independence is relationally greater than dependence.

is only possible through such a being. God is the being of the law; therefore, all legal states are representations of the relation of a person to the divine being, and are lawful as such.

The divine nature is sufficient for the judgment of a person's works. If the legal state agrees with the moral quality, then the judgment is grounded in the person judged, and the lawfulness thereof follows, the law itself judging. If, however, a legal state is not lawful through the person judged, we may appeal to the judge, for if not lawful through the one judged, then it is lawful only through God himself, but legal states are lawful through persons. Therefore, a legal state not lawful through the one judged is lawful through a divine person.

A person is an absolute unity. It is not lawful for one person to execute different judgments upon one and the same person, but one legal state is lawful through one and only one person judging. Therefore, three legal states, and three divine judgments, which are not lawful through Christ's humanity alone, are lawful through three divine persons.

It is lawful for the persons to differ in judgment, through different relations to the persons judged, for each difference of judgment produces an intuition of persons in different relations. There is no law against difference of relation, but for it.[12] Rather, the law is against contrary relations, and difference of judgment, in the same person.[13]

Christ's legal states are intuitions; in them, the universal and the particular are identified. Christ is God manifest in the flesh; his human nature reveals the divine. Therefore, the universal to which the legal states refer is the divine nature, and the particulars are the divine persons. Each legal state is the union of the universal and the particular; therefore, each one thinks the relation of the divine nature to each person, and of the persons to one another.

A human person is an end in itself, whether good or evil, to be justified or condemned accordingly. A divine person is a supreme end in itself, who justifies or condemns for his own sake, whose judgment is lawful, good, and right in itself, and whose manifestation is a supreme end of the moral law. Each person is glorified in his peculiar relation by executing a unique judgment upon Christ.

---

[12] Ex. 20:12.
[13] Jas. 3:10.

For there are three that bear record in heaven, the Father, the Word, and the Holy Ghost: and these three are one. And there are three that bear witness in earth, the spirit, and the water, and the blood: and these three agree in one. 1 John 5:7-8

See also John 5:23, 12:28, 13:31-32, 14, 15:8, 17.

Proposition 1

The Father unconditionally condemns Jesus Christ.

Proof

Christ is condemned, though righteous, therefore unconditionally, not conditional on his person or his works. If not lawful through the person condemned, then lawful only through God, but condemnation is lawful through a person, and this condemnation is unconditional. Therefore, there is a distinct and unconditionally divine person, the Father, who unconditionally condemns Jesus Christ.

Scripture Proof

My God, my God, why hast thou forsaken me? Psalm 22:1

For that he asks why God forsook him, he shows that in himself was no ground of forsaking.

Yet it pleased the LORD to bruise him, he hath put *him* to grief. Isaiah 53:10

Yet, not for sin committed, for "he had done no violence, neither *was any* deceit in his mouth. Yet..." (vs. 10-11); *it pleased,* the end of a particular satisfaction, unconditional; *the LORD*, God categorical, the Father; *to bruise him*, to discipline him, to punish the righteous; *he hath put him to grief*, for God takes no pleasure in the suffering of the wicked, but of the righteous. "Precious in the sight of the LORD *is* the death of his saints" (Psalm 116:15; cf. Ez. 18:23, 32, 33:11).

39

Having predestinated us unto the adoption of children by Jesus Christ to himself, according to the good pleasure of his will, To the praise of the glory of his grace, wherein he hath made us accepted in the beloved. In whom we have redemption through his blood, the forgiveness of sins, according to the riches of his grace… Having made known unto us the mystery of his will, according to his good pleasure which he hath purposed in himself. Ephesians 1:5-7, 9

Which he hath purposed in himself, not in another, to reward the righteous, or punish the wicked, but in himself, to condemn the righteous, and justify the condemned, *to the praise of the glory of his grace… having made known unto us the mystery of his will*, hidden in the Trinity, revealed in Jesus Christ.

For it pleased *the Father* that in him should all fullness dwell, And, having made peace through the blood of his cross, by him to reconcile all things unto himself. Colossians 1:19-20, cf. Jas. 1:17-18, Matt. 11:26, Luke 12:32, Phil. 2:13, Rev. 4:11.

My son, God will provide himself a lamb for a burnt offering. Genesis 22:8, cf. Heb. 11:17-19

What is unlawful without the commandment of God, is lawful through it; it is not lawful for the righteous to be condemned, but through the word of God, who was condemned for the glory of the Father.

See also John 13:31-32, 17:1-5; Phil. 2:11.

Comment

The universal is thought in the particular, the particular through the universal, but the particular, as such, is not universal, and does not refer to any other particular. On the contrary, the particular distinguishes itself from every other particular under a common universal, even those under itself. The particular, through negation, negates reference to any other particular.

The universal refers to the particular, and therefore the particular is the prior condition of the universal's reference; without it, the universal refers to nothing, not even an object. There is no objective condition of the particular, rather, the particular is itself the objective condition of the universal.[14]

It follows that the relation of universal to particular is unconditional.[15] The particular is the subject, the universal is its predicate.[16] In logic, this relationship is called *categorical*.[17] In things, it is called *subsistence* and *inherence*.[18]

The universal and the particular are identified in the singular.[19] The singular is the form of intuition. In the singular, the universal and the particular are identified, though distinguished in thought; therefore, their identity belongs to non-thought, or intuition.[20]

Sensible intuition distinguishes the singular from the universal; therefore, in sensibility, the universal and the particular identified in the singular are also intuited distinctly. The intuitions of the universal and the particular are concepts of intuition, or forms, through which material objects are thought.[21] These forms are time and space.[22] Through them perception is possible.[23]

Time is the universal form of intuition, to which perception, the singular, is particular. The universal of perception is thought itself. Therefore, time is the form of inner sense, of the subject's perception of itself and its thought.[24]

---

[14] Kant, *Pure Reason*, B92-94, B455; Reich, *Completeness*, 34-37, 51-53.

[15] Kant, *Pure Reason*, B224-232; *Metaphysical Foundations of Natural Science*, 39-40.

[16] *Pure Reason*, B98; *Logic*, Section 53. Though convertible, the subject is always conceived of as particular in relation to the predicate, which is universal. This is why, in conversion of a universal affirmative judgment, the subject must be particularized. In a negative judgment, the predicate is conceived of in relation to the subject, not as universal to particular, but as one particular to another, and this is why such judgments may be converted simply.

[17] *Pure Reason*, B95, B98; *Logic*, Sections 23-24.

[18] *Pure Reason*, B102-106.

[19] Reich, *Completeness*, 103-109, and contained references.

[20] Kant, *Pure Reason*, B96-98. The singular and infinite judgments pertain to cognition, not form.

[21] *Pure Reason*, B34-35, B42, B49-51.

[22] *Pure Reason*, B36.

[23] *Pure Reason*, B38-39, B42, B46, B49-51.

[24] *Pure Reason*, B49-51.

Space is the particular form of intuition, to which perception is universal. The particular of perception is the object. Therefore, space is the form of outer sense, of the perception of the object distinct from the subject.[25]

Time is internal to the thinking subject, and to itself;[26] particular times contain others past, and are contained by others future. Time affirms the thinking subject: perception is thought through time, time is intuited in perception. In time, the subject perceives himself perceiving the object.[27]

Space is external to the thinking subject, and to itself;[28] particular spaces exclude one another.[29] Space negates the subject, but affirms the object: perception is thought in space, space is intuited through perception. In space, the subject perceives the world. In time, the subject perceives itself perceiving the world, whereby the existence of the world is demonstrated.[30]

The singular of perception fills time and space.[31] Because they are forms, the filling of time and space is their matter, through which time and space are intuited as totalities.

Time is the universal form of intuition, space is the particular. The filling of time is affirmative; time is the affirmation of perception, and one time of another. The filling of space is negative; space is the negation of perception, and one space of another. In time, one perception affirms another perception; in space, one perception negates another.[32]

Perception is the singular of sensible intuition. The singular is the union of the universal and the particular. The universal and the particular in perception are the forms of time and space. Time and space are therefore concepts of the thinking subject through which sensible intuition is possible. However, perception is not only thought, but also intuition, and contains the identity of the universal and the particular in the intuition of an

[25] Kant, *Pure Reason*, B42-43.
[26] *Pure Reason*, B49-51.
[27] *Pure Reason*, B50-51.
[28] *Pure Reason*, B37-38.
[29] *Pure Reason*, B38, B202-204; *Natural Science*, 33-40.
[30] *Pure Reason*, B272-279.
[31] *Pure Reason*, B182-184, B214.
[32] *Pure Reason*, B218-265; *Natural Science*, 33-40.

object. The universal of perception is sensation, its particular is substance, and their identity[33] is experience.[34]

Time is intuited in perception,[35] as the universal in the particular; therefore, time applies universally to substance: substance is permanent.[36] Perception is intuited through time, and sensation in one time affirms sensation in another; the sensations are distinct, but the underlying subject is the same, and endures, whereas sensation fills particular time, and is transient.[37]

Space is intuited through perception,[38] and perception in space,[39] as the universal in the particular; therefore, perception applies universally to the particular of space. A substance fills a determinate space, limited and bounded, negating and excluding others.[40] Sensation, however, fills universal space, by which space itself is intuited.[41]

If concepts and intuitions are identified, if appearances are regarded as things in themselves, all concepts, and therefore all intuitions and their objects inhere in the thinking subject as mere modifications of its mind, without external existence.[42] As the logical attributes of the thinking subject are hereby exchanged for real ones, so also the real properties of the world are exchanged for logical ones.[43] The subject of thought then contemplates itself as a permanent substance, that is, an immortal soul, and the whole complex of reality is subsumed under the simple unity of the mind.[44] Or else, the thinking subject is reduced to the sum total of its perceptions. This is the paralogism of pure reason.[45]

---

[33] By identity, I do not mean identity of concept, for they are distinct, but identity of intuition, for they are identical in intuition, because the concept of intuition is produced from their identification. Wherefore elsewhere I may refer to this identity as union.

[34] Kant, *Pure Reason*, B126, B165-166, B195-196. Sensation in the subject corresponds to accident in the object.

[35] *Pure Reason*, B225, B233, B257, B455; *Opus Postumum*, 21:549. Neither space nor time can be intuited without perception.

[36] *Pure Reason*, B183, B224-232.

[37] *Pure Reason*, B34, B49-51.

[38] *Opus Postumum*, 21:216, 21:226-229, 21:549.

[39] *Pure Reason*, B38-39, B42.

[40] *Natural Science*, 33-74.

[41] I do not mean to negate the possibility of an empty space, only that an empty space is that which lacks a substance. It need not follow that all space is not full of a substance purely perceptive, i.e. a medium, but this is not the place.

[42] *Pure Reason*, A366-380, B416-418.

[43] *Pure Reason*, A338-405, B406-432.

[44] *Pure Reason*, A348-351, A366-380, B407-408, B409-411.

[45] *Pure Reason*, B396-398. As in Berkeley or Hume.

The thinking subject is one, simple, subject, and problematic; these are its logical attributes, and they are subjectively valid.[46] The thinking subject is not the ground of an intuition, but only of concepts, and of the application of concepts to given intuitions. The thinking subject does not therefore possess any objective reality of its own.[47]

If, however, the thinking subject thinks a concept through which intuitions may be produced, the subject gives objective reality to itself, as the ground of the objects produced, yea, as producing an intuition of itself.[48] This concept is the moral law, which contains within itself the ground of an intuition. The thinking subject as moral is therefore objectively real in a practical way, for the moral law contains within itself an intuition as to its groundedness, that is, practically. Accordingly, the intuition of the thinking subject may be subsumed under time and applied to space, yielding two doctrines of the appearance of a thing in itself: the immortality of the soul,[49] and its presence.[50]

The divine unity is revealed in the harmony of diverse judgments executed upon Christ. A legal state is the relation of a person to the law, of a particular to a universal. It follows that a legal state is an intuition, and Christ's legal states are singular representations of the divine nature. The universal of each is the divine nature revealed. The particular of each is the divine person to which the nature refers. The singular itself is the divine judgment. A person is an absolute unity; therefore, one judgment is to one person only. There are three judgments, therefore three divine persons.

The singular contains the universal and the particular identified, therefore also the relation of the universal to its particular. The judgments are different, and contain different relations of one nature to different persons. The persons are not distinguished by difference of nature, but by difference of relation to one nature, for the three possess one and the same nature, but a person subsists in its relation to the predicate. If, then, the subject is not distinguished by its predicate, then it must be distinguished by its relation to the predicate.

---

[46] Kant, *Pure Reason*, A348-381, B406-413, B418-421, B426-427.

[47] *Pure Reason*, A381-384, A396-405, B418-426, B428-432; *Practical Reason*, 5:6-7, 5:15-16, 5:19-21, 5:42-50. The thinking subject, as such, for it may be determined through practical reason.

[48] *Pure Reason*, B424-426, B430-432; *Practical Reason*, 5:3-6, 5:46-57, 5:132-138, 5:142-146.

[49] Ez. 18:4; *Pure Reason*, B424-426, B838-844; *Practical Reason*, 5:122-124.

[50] Gen. 2:7; *Pure Reason*, A384-396, B427-428.

There are three and only three relations by which the persons may be distinguished: independence, dependence, and interdependence. A person is one; one relation is for one legal judgment; and there are three and only three legal judgments. There are therefore three and only three divine persons.

The proofs given deduce the persons from the judgments. The persons being given, the judgments may also be deduced from them. Christ's condemnation is the negation of his standing before the law. Christ is condemned not for sin, but for the negation of sin, for the negation of sin is divine, because an inwardly lawful being is one that cannot sin.

Wherefore also: the Father possesses the divine nature independently. Independence is the negation of any prior condition. Negation in God is condemnation. Therefore, to the Father belongs unconditional condemnation.

Proposition 2

The Son of God submits himself to the condemnation of the Father through his nonlegal righteousness.

Proof

Christ is righteous, though condemned. If righteous, but not legally, then nonlegally righteous as God, though condemned as man. However, the lawfulness of his submission to condemnation depends upon the lawfulness of the condemnation to which he submits, and is lawful through a person, as the other; therefore, this person depends upon the other, and Jesus Christ is the Son of God. Thus, the Son of God submits himself to the condemnation of the Father through his nonlegal righteousness.

Scripture Proof

> Who did no sin, neither was guile found in his mouth: Who, when he was reviled, reviled not again; when he suffered, he threatened not; but committed *himself* to him that judgeth righteously: Who his own self bore our sins in his own body on the tree... 1 Peter 2:22-24

O my Father, if it be possible, let this cup pass from me, neverthe-less not as I will, but as thou *wilt*. Matthew 26:39, cf. Mark 14:36, Luke 22:42

O my Father, if this cup may not pass away from me, except I drink it, thy will be done. Matthew 26:42

Then Jesus said to Peter, Put up thy sword into the sheath: the cup which my Father hath given me, shall I not drink it? John 18:11

Christ drank the cup of God's wrath willingly, and so it passed away from him. The wrath of God is satisfied by the submission of the Son. "A soft answer turneth away wrath" (Proverbs 15:1).

Then answered Jesus and said unto them, Verily, verily, I say unto you, The Son can do nothing of himself, but what he seeth the Father do: for what things soever he doeth, these also doeth the Son likewise. John 5:19

When ye have lifted up the Son of Man, then shall ye know that I am *he*, and *that* I do nothing of myself; but as my Father hath taught me, I speak these things. And he that sent me is with me: the Father hath not left me alone; for I do always those things that please him. John 8:28-29

Therefore doth my Father love me, because I lay down my life, that I might take it again. No man taketh it from me, but I lay it down of myself. I have power to lay it down, and I have power to take it again. This commandment have I received of my Father. John 10:15-18

Now is the Son of man glorified, and God is glorified in him. If God be glorified in him, God shall also glorify him in himself, and shall straightway glorify him. John 13:31-32

Father, the hour is come; glorify thy Son, that thy Son also may glorify thee: As thou hast given him power over all flesh, that he should give eternal life to as many as thou hast given him. And this is life eternal, that they might know thee the only true God, and Jesus Christ whom thou hast sent. John 17:1-3

Jesus bears his Father's cross, for what the Father does, the Son does like-wise: as the Father condemns the Son, so the Son bears the condemnation of the Father, for it is one with God to smite, and to be smitten, that men may know the Father through the Son.

> God, who at sundry times and in divers manners spake in time past unto the fathers by the prophets, Hath in these last days spo-ken unto us by *his* Son, whom he hath appointed heir of all things, by whom also he made the worlds; who being the brightness of *his* glory, and the express image of his person, and upholding all things by the word of his power, when he had by himself purged our sins, sat down on the right hand of the Majesty on high. He-brews 1:1-3

Who is like God, but God?[51] The Son of God, who is God.

Comment

A hypothetical judgment is the relation of one categorical judgment to another.[52] This connection is twofold. If the subject of each categorical judgment is the same, the predicate proceeds from particular to universal, as from subject to predicate.[53] If the predicate is the same, the subject pro-ceeds from universal to particular, as from predicate to subject.[54]

A categorical judgment relates predicate to subject. The predicate lies in the subject; therefore, the relation of predicate to subject also lies in the subject.

---

[51] A comparison distinguishes, and God is an absolute unity. Therefore, nothing compares to God, but God himself, one person to another. The Word *of God* compares to God, and is a divine person. Likewise, Is. 40:18, 55:11, and Ps. 33:6 refer to the Son.

[52] Kant, *Pure Reason*, B95, 98-99; *Logic*, Section 25; Reich, *Completeness*, 51-53. Originally, for categorical judgments are the only material available from which to form a hypothet-ical, but afterwards any judgment may be employed.

[53] "If Socrates is a man, then Socrates is mortal." Man is to mortal as particular to univer-sal.

[54] "If all men are mortal, then Socrates is mortal." Man is to Socrates as universal to par-ticular.

A hypothetical judgment relates ground to consequence. This relation is not in either, or else the judgment is categorical. Therefore, the hypothetical relation is mediated by another categorical judgment.[55] The mediating judgment is universal to one, particular to the other, and operates through a mediating concept, whether subject or predicate, universal to the particular, and particular to the universal.[56]

If the subject is constant and the predicate varies, the mediating concept is in the subject, and the judgment proceeds from particular to universal. The mediating judgment is universal to the antecedent, and particular to the consequent.

If the subject varies and the predicate is constant, the mediating concept is in the predicate, and the judgment proceeds from universal to particular. The mediating judgment is particular to the antecedent, and universal to the consequent.

In a categorical judgment, concepts relate to one another as predicate to subject. Intuitions subsumed under concepts are cases thereof, and stand in the same relation, not logically, but really, as subsistence and inherence.

In logic, subject and predicate are concepts, and are convertible,[57] because logic thinks the form of thought only, and leaves the matter undetermined.[58] In reality, however, subject and predicate are intuitions, inconvertible, because the matter is thought together with the form. The relation of inherence to subsistence is therefore a determination of the universal and the particular to the functions of predicate and subject in an intuition.[59]

A categorical judgment is a relation of concepts. The relation of concepts is itself a concept.[60] It follows that categorical judgments relate to one another, like as subject and predicate. This is the hypothetical relation.

---

[55] In the first example, the mediating judgment is "All men are mortal"; in the second, it is "Socrates is a man."

[56] In both examples, the mediating concept is the same: "man" is universal to "Socrates," particular to "mortality." In the first example, the mediating concept is the subject of the mediating judgment: "all men are mortal"; in the second, the mediating concept is its predicate: "Socrates is a man."

[57] Kant, *Pure Reason*, B128-129, B185-187. "All men are mortal" converts to "some mortals are men."

[58] *Pure Reason*, B74-79, B83-84; *Logic*, Sections 19, 44.

[59] See footnote 58.

[60] Reich, *Completeness*, 51-53.

Furthermore, intuitions subsumed under concepts relate to one another hypothetically. This is called *causality* and *dependence*.[61]

The unit of perception is a substance with its accidents. Time distinguishes one perception from another. The understanding relates one time to another through causality and dependence. Every perception is grounded in another perception, and is the ground of yet another; prior to one, posterior to another.[62]

The temporal order of causes and effects owes itself to the subject's perception of himself in the perception of an object. Time is the form of inner sense; therefore, what is prior in thought is also prior in time, and the temporal order of perceptions is from ground to consequence.

If, in a causal connection, the subject is constant and the accident varies, the understanding proceeds from particular to universal, and the mediating concept from universal to particular. The universal is past, the particular is future, and the present is singular. The future is intuited through the past, as the particular is thought through the universal. The past motion of a body, in the absence of other forces, determines its future position.

If the subject varies, and the predicate is constant, the understanding proceeds from universal to particular, the mediating concept from particular to universal, and the past is intuited in the future, as the universal is thought in the particular. The accident of one substance is transferred to another, the quick to the slow, the hot to the cold. In the absence of other forces, the past state is deducible from the future.

In either case, the present is the singular in which the past and the future are united, and is the mediating concept of a hypothetical relation. The present is perception in time, the past is its ground, and the future is its consequent.

The antinomies[63] of reason follow the form of hypothetical syllogisms.[64] Those of the constitution[65] of appearances proceed as follows. Every boundary divides particular space, or time, from universal.[66] The

---

[61] Kant, *Pure Reason*, B102-106.

[62] *Pure Reason*, B232-256.

[63] *Pure Reason*, B432-595.

[64] *Pure Reason*, B377-380, B432-433. According to Kant, there are three kinds of problems of pure reason, one modeled after the syllogisms of each relational form of judgment: categorical, hypothetical, and disjunctive.

[65] *Pure Reason*, B220-223, B557-560.

[66] *Pure Reason*, B454-461. Kant's first antinomy.

parts of bodies are bodies made of smaller parts, and form a boundary between the parts and the whole.[67]

The antinomies of the regulation[68] of appearances also proceed hypothetically. Every cause is also the effect of another cause, receding infinitely to causes bound, or finitely to causes free.[69] Events that follow from their causes are either contingent upon their causes, or because of them, necessary; therefore, all events are contingent, or else there is a necessary being, whether that being is the series of contingent events itself, or a being outside the series.[70]

These are the four antinomies of human reason. The constitutive antinomies are insoluble, because the preceding term is ever determined to both of two mutually exclusive terms.[71] Every given space is bounded by a space particular, or universal; every body is made of parts that are bodies, or not. In these series, neither finitude nor infinitude is adequate to experience, which gives the progression[72] from one perception to another, and not the other itself.[73]

However, the regulative antinomies are soluble, because the prior condition may be different in kind from the conditioned, that the alternatives be not mutually exclusive.[74] An event is an object of thought as well as an object of intuition, and may therefore have an intelligible cause in addition to the sensible, namely, the free and rational agent.[75] The events of this world are contingent among appearances, but they may also have their

---

[67] Kant, *Pure Reason*, B462-471. Kant's second antinomy.
[68] See footnote 66.
[69] *Pure Reason*, B472-479. Kant's third antinomy.
[70] *Pure Reason*, B480-489. Kant's fourth antinomy.
[71] *Pure Reason*, B530-560.
[72] *Pure Reason*, B536-543.
[73] *Pure Reason*, B530-535. A statement may be false in two ways. Either the concept is coherent, but does not agree with the intuition, or the concept is self-contradictory. A contradiction cannot be thought, let alone an intuition corresponding to it. Likewise, the statement, "This statement is false," is false, not because the opposite is true, but because it has no meaning. The Jews rightly told Jesus that self-attesting statements are false, to which he replied, that his statements are not self-attesting, because he proceeds from the Father (John 8:12-18). Likewise, any complex question, if it contains a false supposition, is false. The question, "Is space infinite or finite?" is such a question. The answer is, space is neither finite nor infinite, because these respect wholes, and time and space are not intuited as wholes, but as manifolds.
[74] *Pure Reason*, B560-593.
[75] *Pure Reason*, B560-586, Bxxiv-xxx.

necessity from an absolutely necessary being.[76] The former pertain to appearances, the latter to things in themselves.[77] The alternatives are therefore not mutually exclusive. One is required by theoretical reason, the other by practical reason.[78]

The moral law requires the subject to produce an intuition in agreement with its concept. The particular of an intuition in agreement with the concept of the thinking subject is *happiness*; the thinking faculty as ground of the possibility of happiness is *desire*; thought as means to this end is *will*.[79] The moral law is the ground of happiness; therefore, freedom is the ability of the self to will one's own happiness through the moral law.[80]

The hypothetical relation of causality and dependence is the form of the Son's relation to the Father.[81] The Father is to the divine nature as particular to universal, and the Son to the Father; therefore, the Father is God independently, the Son in dependence on the Father, and because the divine nature is universal to both, from the Father to the Son, the Son is one God with the Father.

The divine nature is universal, not particular, but inheres in the persons, and therefore also in its relation to the persons, as in a relation. The Son is God, and the begetting of the Son is divine: it is one, eternal, &etc. He is "the *only begotten* Son" (John 3:16). One word, μονογενη.

In the submission of the Son to condemnation lies the condemnation to which he submits. The lawfulness of the one depends upon the lawfulness of the other, and the person of the one upon the person of the other, because the judgments are representations of the persons. Therefore, Jesus Christ depends upon the Father, that is, he is the Son of God. And because the lawfulness of his submission contains within itself the lawfulness of the condemnation to which he submits, it is one and the same inward lawfulness by which the Father condemns, and the Son submits, and the Father and the Son are one God.

The Son depends upon the Father. The Father is God unconditionally. The Father's independence is a negation of dependence, which is affirmed

---

[76] Kant, *Pure Reason*, B586-593.

[77] *Pure Reason*, B572-586, B591-593.

[78] *Pure Reason*, Bxxiv-xxxv, B575-585, B825-847; *Practical Reason*, 5:114-115.

[79] *Groundwork*, 4:412-413; *Judgment*, ak. 172, 220.

[80] Gen. 2:16-17; Matt. 5:29-30; Jas. 1:25.

[81] "Cause" refers to time; as such, it does not describe the begetting of the Son. Nevertheless, the form of this category, which is dependence, does.

in the Son. To the Son it belongs to affirm the negation thought in the Father. Affirmation of a negation is infinity, and infinity in the divine nature is nonlegal righteousness; therefore, through his nonlegal righteousness the Son submits himself to the condemnation of the Father.

It is not lawful for a righteous man to be condemned without his consent, for the law requires every man to be respected as an end in himself, and not as a mere means.[82] If that man's consent cannot be the ground of the condemnation, because the condemnation is unconditional, then the condemnation must be the ground of that righteous man's consent.[83] God is the author of Christ's consent to condemnation, because he is the author of his person, and through his submission thereunto the Son is glorified in his dependence on the Father.

Neither is it lawful for a righteous man to consent to condemnation, because condemnation regards a man as wicked. Nevertheless, it is lawful for Christ, because he gives his consent to condemnation in dependence on its author, not through the law, but above it, through his nonlegal righteousness, according to the divine nature manifested in human flesh.

Therefore, the condemnation of Christ is lawful because of the intuition it produces of the Father, and the submission of Christ to condemnation is lawful because of the intuition it produces of the Son.

Proposition 3

The Holy Spirit justifies Jesus Christ in his submission to the unconditional condemnation of the Father.

Proof

Christ is righteous, and he is a man, therefore, Christ is a righteous man. God justifies the righteous, therefore, God justifies Christ. Christ's justification is lawful through both the righteousness of Christ's submission to condemnation, and the lawfulness of the condemnation to which he submits. Both the condemnation and Christ's submission to it are lawful through persons; therefore, the justification of Christ is also lawful through a person, but that justification depends upon both the Father's

---

[82] Kant, *Groundwork*, 4:428-431.
[83] *Practical Reason*, 5:113-119.

condemnation and the Son's submission. Thus, the justifying person depends upon both the Father and the Son, who depend upon one another in his procession. This is the Holy Spirit. Therefore, the Holy Spirit justifies Jesus Christ in his submission to condemnation.

Scripture Proof

To better understand the verses cited, let these four principles be understood.

First, the divine nature is absolutely one and invisible. Any plurality or visibility divine must therefore be spoken of the persons. E.g. Genesis 1:1-3.

Second, an attribute of God, distinct from God, refers to an attribute in a distinct person. This follows from the first principle. If the attribute is really different from the nature, and not merely logically distinguished, that is, if they are present in different divine judgments, then the attribute refers to a distinct person, as its distinguishing condition. An attribute distinct from God himself is an attribute inhering in a distinct person. And since that person possesses the divine attribute, he possesses the divine nature, and is a divine person, e.g. Is. 9:3, Rev. 8:4. The same reasoning applies to figures and instruments of God, such as the hand of God, the eyes and ears of God, the shadow of his wings, the place and presence of God, God as strong tower and refuge, and others, as often found in the psalms.

Third, the judgments differ, but the unity of the nature and the relations of the persons allow the judgment of one to be imputed to another, as by means of the first. The Father justifies Christ by the Holy Spirit, even as Christ offers himself to God through the Spirit, because the Holy Spirit is the Spirit of the Father and of the Son.

Likewise, the persons may be denoted by their relations or modalities. The Father is God, categorical; the Son begotten of the Father is the Word of God, God manifest in the flesh; and the Spirit is the attribute or instrument of God, proceeding from God.

Fourth, if by these marks a person may be understood, he must be. Not only does the divine unity require that real distinctions in God be referred to the persons, but also through them our salvation is possible. God speaks to sinners, commanding them to repent and believe, promising them eternal life. He does not therefore tell us only of his nature, by which we ought to be destroyed, but of the persons, through whom we may be saved, for

God saves not by his nature as such, but in accordance with his nature dwelling in, and exercised by the persons. What is the predicate, but not the predicate? The subject. What is the nature of God, but not the nature of God? A divine person. Wherefore they may speak of the nature, but they must speak of the persons.

> And without controversy great is the mystery of godliness: God was manifest in the flesh, justified in the Spirit. 1 Timothy 3:16

Christ is manifest in the flesh through his condemnation, and in his submission thereto he is *justified in the Spirit.*

> For Christ also hath once suffered for sins, the just for the unjust, that he might bring us to God, being put to death in the flesh, but quickened by the Spirit. 1 Peter 3:18

Put to death in the flesh, condemned in the flesh; *quickened by the Spirit*, justified by the Spirit.

> How much more shall the blood of Christ, who through the eternal Spirit offered himself without spot to God, purge your conscience from dead works to serve the living God? Hebrews 9:14

Without spot, righteous; *to God,* legally righteous; *through the eternal Spirit* justified.[84]

> Watch and pray, that ye enter not into temptation. The spirit indeed *is* willing, but the flesh *is* weak. Matthew 26:41

The spirit indeed is willing, willing Christ's will in him; *but the flesh is weak*, that he should rely on the Spirit to justify him in his submission to wrath, for his prayer before is,

---

[84] Those who say that "the Spirit" refers to the divine nature of Christ are refuted thusly. The divine nature of Christ is the divine nature of the Holy Spirit; therefore, the divine nature of Christ must refer distinctly to his person, but the person of Christ is never called spirit. The only divine person called "spirit" is the Holy Spirit.

O my Father, if it be possible, let this cup pass from me: nevertheless not as I will, but as thou *wilt.* Matthew 26:39

But we see Jesus, who was made a little lower than the angels for the suffering of death, crowned with glory and honor; that he by the grace of God should taste death for every man. Hebrews 2:9

Taste death, willingly die; *by the grace of God,* the "Spirit of grace" (Hebrews 10:29).

For his anger *endureth but* a moment, in his favor *is* life: weeping may endure for a night, but joy *cometh* in the morning. And in my prosperity I said, I shall never be moved. LORD, by thy favor thou hast made my mountain to stand strong: thou didst hide thy face, *and* I was troubled. Psalm 30:5-7

For his anger, the Father's, *endureth but a moment, in his favor,* the Holy Spirit, *is life.*

My God, my God, why hast thou forsaken me? *why art thou so* far from helping me, *and from* the words of my roaring? O my God, I cry in the day time, and thou hearest not; and in the night season, and am not silent. Psalm 22:1-2

God heard him not, save with his Spirit.

Now know I that the LORD saveth his anointed; he will hear him from his holy heaven with the saving strength of his right hand. Psalm 20:6

The saving strength of his right hand, the Holy Spirit; *the LORD,* the Father; *his anointed,* the Son.

Into thine hand I commit my spirit; thou hast redeemed me, O LORD God of truth. Psalm 31:5

Thine hand, the instrument of salvation.

In thee, O LORD, do I put my trust; let me never be ashamed: deliver me in thy righteousness. Bow down thine ear to me; deliver me speedily: be thou my strong rock, for an house of defence to save me. Psalm 31:1-2

The prayers of one forsaken by God, who yet trusts in him.

Have mercy upon me, O LORD, for I am in trouble: mine eye is consumed with grief, *yea*, my soul and my belly. For my life is spent with grief, and my years with sighing: my strength faileth because of mine iniquity, and my bones are consumed. Psalm 31:9-10

Yet,

I will be glad and rejoice in thy mercy; for thou hast considered my trouble; thou hast known my soul in adversities... My times *are* in thy hand: deliver me from the hand of mine enemies, and from them that persecute me. Make thy face to shine upon thy servant: save me for thy mercies' sake... *Oh* how great *is* thy goodness, which thou hast laid up for them that fear thee; *which* thou hast wrought for them that trust in thee before the sons of men! Thou shalt hide them in the secret of thy presence from the pride of man: thou shalt keep them secretly in a pavilion from the strife of tongues. Blessed *be* the LORD: for he hath shewed me his marvellous kindness in a strong city. For I said in my haste, I am cut off from before thine eyes: nevertheless thou heardest the voice of my supplications when I cried unto thee. Psalm 31:7, 15-16, 19-22

Forsaken of God, but not of his Spirit.

Be merciful unto me, O God, be merciful unto me: for my soul trusteth in thee: yea, in the shadow of thy wings will I make my refuge, until *these* calamities be overpast. I will cry unto God most high; unto God that performeth *all things* for me. He shall send from heaven, and save me *from* the reproach of him that would swallow me up. Selah. God shall send forth his mercy and his truth. Psalm 57:1-3

God troubled him, but he took refuge in *the shadow of his wings, his mercy and his truth*, which God should *send forth*, not as such, but in the Spirit of mercy and truth, who proceeds from the Father and the Son, one wing of mercy, the other of truth.

> Shew thy marvellous lovingkindness, O thou that savest by thy right hand them which put their trust *in thee* from those that rise up *against them*. Keep me as the apple of the eye, hide me under the shadow of thy wings. Psalm 17:7-8

> For in the time of trouble he shall hide me in his pavilion: in the secret of his tabernacle shall he hide me; he shall set me up upon a rock. Psalm 27:5

> O God, thou *art* my God; early will I seek thee: my soul thirsteth for thee, my flesh longeth for thee in a dry and thirsty land, where no water is… Because thou hast been my help, therefore in the shadow of thy wings will I rejoice. My soul followeth hard after thee: thy right hand upholdeth me. Psalm 63:1, 7-8

> He that dwelleth in the secret place of the most High shall abide under the shadow of the Almighty. I will say of the Lord, *He is* my refuge and my fortress: my God; in him will I trust. Surely he shall deliver thee from the snare of the fowler, *and* from the noisome pestilence. He shall cover thee with his feathers, and under his wings shalt thou trust: his truth *shall be thy* shield and buckler. Psalm 91:1-4

In the shadow of thy wings is relief from the wrath of God, and *in the secret place of the most High* is justification of his submission to the Father.

> And walk in love, as Christ also hath loved us, and hath given himself for us an offering and a sacrifice to God for a sweet smelling savour. Ephesians 5:2, cf. Gen. 8:20-21, Lev. 1:9, 13, 17, &etc.

A sweet smelling savour, for the Spirit is the breath of God,[85] through whom the Father receives the sacrifice of the Son.

> Whither shall I go from thy spirit? or whither shall I flee from thy presence? If I ascend up into heaven, thou *art* there: if I make my bed in hell, behold, thou *art there. If* I take the wings of the morning, *and* dwell in the uttermost parts of the sea; even there shall thy hand lead me, and thy right hand shall hold me. Psalm 139:7-10

If I make my bed in hell, to rest in heavenly wrath; *even there shall thy hand lead me, and thy right hand shall hold me,* to comfort him in woe, he gives him his Spirit.

Wherefore, God receives the sacrifice of his Son through the Holy Spirit, even as Christ through the Holy Spirit offers himself to God.

Comment

The disjunctive form of judgment relates whole to part.[86] The relation of concepts is itself a concept; therefore, the relation of the categorical to the hypothetical is also a concept, that is, a relation of concepts, or of relations.[87] The categorical form contains negation of a prior condition. The hypothetical form contains the infinite, the affirmation of something besides. The disjunctive form is therefore a categorical judgment that contains within itself a hypothetical relation of its parts, an affirmation of one through the negation of the others.

The mediating concept of a disjunctive judgment is the universal, under which stand several particulars. Each particular contains the universal within itself, and distinguishes itself, and the universal in it, from all the others. The universal in the particular is a categorical judgment; the relation of each categorical judgment to the others is hypothetical; and the universal mediates between the diverse particulars and their judgments.

Affirmation flows from negation and infinity, for infinity affirms a quality outside negation, namely, affirmation. Infinity is formally identical to affirmation, and in logic, affirmation and negation are infinite to one

---

[85] Gen. 1:1-3; Ps. 33:6.
[86] Kant, *Pure Reason*, B98-99; *Logic*, Sections 23, 27-29.
[87] *Pure Reason*, B98-99, B111; Reich, *Completeness*, 54-56.

another.[88] Therefore, the negative may also be affirmed through the affirmation's negation. This is a disjunctive judgment.

Affirmation is therefore also the mediating concept of a disjunctive judgment, as negation of a categorical, and infinity of a hypothetical. The universal applies to one or the other particular. This is an affirmative judgment.[89] The particular is object to the universal; if then the universal refers to an object, it refers to one of the particulars under the universal.

Pure logic is not the form of things, but of thought. In logic, quantity and quality are composed of two forms each.[90] The third forms, which are combinations of the former, belong not to pure logic, but applied, for they are the forms of the intuition of an object.[91] However, relations of concepts refer to objects, even logical ones.[92] A relation is the reference of one concept to another in the identity of a concept.[93] A relation is a union of distinct concepts, and contains the form of intuition in reference to an object. Even logical relations refer to logical objects. It follows that opposite relations combine into distinct forms of thought, and the division of relations is threefold.[94] Thus, the disjunctive form arises out of the categorical and the hypothetical, as a distinct act of judgment.[95]

Applied to sensible intuition, the disjunctive form of judgment thinks the plurality of intuitions within a common unity. Experience is a totality whose parts determine one another through their reciprocal causality.[96]

---

[88] In logic, affirmation and negation are indeterminate, lacking content; wherefore in a disjunctive judgment they are relative terms, unless the judgment itself is purely logical, as an object is either red or not red.

[89] Kant, *Logic*, Section 29. For example, the book is some color. Therefore, the book is either red, or blue, or yellow, etc.

[90] *Pure Reason*, B96-98; Reich, *Completeness*, 105-109.

[91] Kant, *Pure Reason*, B77-79.

[92] *Pure Reason*, B128-129, A103-105, A108-110, B137, B140-142, A248-253; Immanuel Kant, *Prolegomena to Any Future Metaphysics*, ed. by Lewis White Beck, trans. by Paul Carus (New York: Macmillan/Library of Liberal Arts, 1950), Section 39, footnote; Reich, *Completeness*, 28-29, 65-67, 87-92. A logical object is what is thought through the form of thought. It therefore signifies the relation of thought to the concept of an object, and the logical relations present logical objects.

[93] Kant, *Pure Reason*, B92-94, B98-99; *Logic*, Section 17, 23; Reich, *Completeness*, 69-83.

[94] Kant, *Pure Reason*, B96-101; Reich, *Completeness*, 101-109.

[95] Kant, *Pure Reason*, B98-99, B111; *Logic*, Section 24.

[96] *Pure Reason*, B111-113, B256-265.

Simultaneity is the temporal schema[97] of this interdependence, because the mutual causality of substances is represented through a common time.[98]

In the subject, sensations mutually exclude one another,[99] as particulars under a common universal, but in the object, these same sensations are included in one experience through the application of the disjunctive form of judgment to intuition.[100] In intuition, the universal is identified with the particular, and contains the particulars within itself, and therefore each particular affirms the others, and is affirmed by them. Objects of sensible intuition determine one another's accidents, not their substance or existence.[101] The state of one is indeed negative to the other,[102] and in the subject, one intuition excludes another,[103] but in the object, the substances do not destroy, but mutually depend on one another, as parts of a whole, so that one may proceed in consciousness from one part to another, as from cause to effect, save that here, one may proceed from any part to any other, and vice versa, at any time, because of the simultaneity through which their mutual causality is applied to the whole of intuition.[104]

God is thought itself, a universal being, the ground of all that is thought, for thought is universal to all particular thinking subjects, and as object, to the objects of thought. This is the logical conception of God; the theoretical conception of God is that of self-subsisting reason as the ground of all that is.[105] The theoretical is as the logical applied to intuition.

The logical conception of God does not ask whether he exists, for he is merely thought; the theoretical conception of God asks whether he is,

---

[97] Kant, *Pure Reason*, B176-187. A schema is a combination of two opposite representations, whereby one is subsumed under the other, through their mutual agreement with a third. The schemata of appearances are in time, because time is the form of inner intuition, that is, of the intuition of the thinking subject and its thoughts, in which concept and intuition are identified.

[98] *Pure Reason*, B183-184, B256-260.

[99] *Pure Reason*, A98-100.

[100] *Pure Reason*, B111-113.

[101] *Pure Reason*, B229-232, B259-260.

[102] For example, change in momentum is negative in one object, positive in the other; or heat gained is equal to heat lost.

[103] *Pure Reason*, A98-110. The intuition of one object in one time excludes the intuition of any other object in that same time, for the degree of focus spent on one object is lost to all the others, by the nature of focus. One intuition includes the others in the object, as its determining ground, but not in the sensation itself.

[104] *Pure Reason*, B258-259.

[105] *Pure Reason*, B697-732.

for he is the ground of all that is; but it may not answer. Nevertheless, it follows from the theoretical conception of God, that he is one, simple, immaterial, omnipresent, eternal, omniscient, &etc.[106]

The theoretical conception of God does not prove his existence.[107] God is indeed a being whose concept contains its intuition, for within him lies the ground of all that is, but this concept of God does not contain its intuition within itself, for this reason: the universality of the concept is such as to exclude all particularity, and therefore any intuition, in which universality might be united with particularity.

Thus, the intuition of God cannot be found within this conception of God, but neither can it found outside of a particular conception of God, by the definition of God. Therefore, the universal and indeterminate concept of God, as self-subsisting reason, and the ground of all that is, is an idea, a concept without a corresponding intuition.[108]

There are three theoretical arguments for the existence of God: the ontological, the cosmological, and the physico-theological.[109] The ontological argument seeks to demonstrate God's existence merely from the concept of God, as that of a being whose concept contains its own intuition. The cosmological argues from an intuition to another intuition in identity with the concept of God, as first cause of the world; and the physico-theological offers an identity of concept and intuition that is itself a concept and an intuition of God, as ground of the order and harmony of the world.[110] These arguments fail to demonstrate the existence of God, as thought itself, because this conception of God excludes an intuition in which his being might be given.[111]

The ontological argument proceeds as follows: the concept of God contains its own intuition, because existence is a necessary predicate of a perfect being, and the being so conceived must exist.[112] I answer, it is true

---

[106] Kant, *Pure Reason*, B595-611.

[107] *Pure Reason*, B611-630.

[108] *Pure Reason*, B368-377, B383-385, B595-611, B697-732. Not an idea only, but an ideal, "an individual thing determinable or even determined by the idea alone," "containing all empirical reality within itself" (*Pure Reason*, B596, B610).

[109] *Pure Reason*, B618-619.

[110] *Pure Reason*, B620-658.

[111] *Pure Reason*, B611-618.

[112] Rene Descartes, "The Meditations Concerning First Philosophy," in *Philosophical Essays*, trans. by Laurence J. Lafleur (New York: Macmillan/Library of Liberal Arts, 1960), Third Meditation. Although Anselm's formulation is favored, Descartes' is clearer.

that the concept of God is identical to his intuition, but because man distinguishes intuitions from concepts, man does not intuit God through his concept, but conceives of him only, and therefore no demonstration of God's existence is possible from the theoretical conception of God.[113]

The cosmological argument is, there is a first cause of the world, and that first cause is God. I answer, the intuition of God must agree with the concept, as that of a being whose concept contains within itself its own intuition, but God as first cause of the world contains the intuition of God outside the concept, in distinction therefrom. Thus, no argument is possible from the existence of the world.[114]

The physico-theological argument is, there is a cause of the harmony of purposes in the world, and this cause is God; that the order of the world is expressive of a being that exists through his concept. I answer, the agreement of the intuition of God with his concept is contained in the concept, and in the intuition in identity with the concept, and cannot therefore be intuited in the external world, and no identity of concept and intuition can be intuited in the world. Thus, no argument is possible from the order and harmony of the world.[115]

The ontological argument fails on subjective grounds, namely, the distinction between concepts and intuitions. The cosmological argument fails on objective grounds, namely, the disagreement between the intuition presented and the concept of the being to be intuited. The physico-theological argument fails on both subjective and objective grounds, because it supposes to intuit the identity of a concept and an intuition outside the being to which it belongs. With these three arguments, all bases for a theoretical demonstration of the existence of God have been exhausted. It is impossible for theoretical reason to prove the existence of God.[116]

Thought itself is the object of thought, but not yet the thought of an object. If, then, thought refers a priori to an object, the concept of God is determinable by reference to this object. Once determined, the existence of God may be demonstrated accordingly.[117]

---

[113] Kant, *Pure Reason*, B620-630.
[114] *Pure Reason*, B631-648.
[115] *Pure Reason*, B648-658.
[116] *Pure Reason*, Bxiv-xv, Bxxviii-xxxv, B659-670.
[117] *Practical Reason*, 5:15-16.

Practical reason determines the concept of God.[118] The thinking subject determines itself to produce an intuition in agreement with its concept. The person's object is happiness through the moral law. God is the union of righteousness and blessedness, the ground of the happiness of his creatures in their obedience to the moral law. Thus, for man to find happiness in obedience to the law, there must be a God to reward every man according to his works.

God is an inwardly lawful being. This concept contains within itself the intuition not given, but to be produced. Practical reason prescribes an intuition in which obedience and happiness are united. If this intuition is given, it follows that God exists. Because the intuition is not given, but to be produced, this conception of God does not suffice for theoretical, but only for practical proof. What is required, must be presupposed possible, and the conditions of this possibility taken for granted.[119] The existence of God is the necessary condition of the possibility of man's final end. It is therefore necessary from a practical point of view.[120]

The proposition, God exists, is theoretical.[121] If the truth of this proposition is a requirement of practical reason, it may be demanded of theoretical, and that for the sake of practical, for the intuition to be produced must itself be received by theoretical reason in order to have been produced by practical.[122]

Practical reason must therefore be subsumed under theoretical.[123] All subsumption requires a common element.[124] If the common element is common to each member, then the subsumption is analytic, and the conclusion follows logically.[125] If, however, the common element is not contained in each member, it must be contained in a third, and the agreement

---

[118] Kant, *Pure Reason*, B661-662, B836; *Practical Reason*, 5:3-5, 5:132-146.

[119] *Practical Reason*, 5:122-126, 5:134-136, 5:142-143.

[120] Deut. 29:29; Ps. 14, 53; Jas. 1:26-27; *Pure Reason*, B661-662, B848-859; *Practical*, 5:124-126, 5:142-143.

[121] *Practical Reason*, 5:119-121, 5:134-138.

[122] *Pure Reason*, A108; *Judgment*, ak. 195-196; Gress, *Harmony*, 3-4.

[123] Kant, *Judgment*, ak. 176-179, 195-198, 286-291, 338-346; Gress, *Harmony*, 5-6, 14-16, 24-25. The whole faculty under the other, and therefore the objects of the one under the objects of the other.

[124] Kant, *Pure Reason*, B176-187.

[125] *Pure Reason*, B187-193.

of each member with the third.[126] This is the course followed by all real subsumption of an intuition under a concept.[127]

Theoretical reason applies concepts to intuitions; practical reason produces intuitions through concepts. Hence, theoretical reason provides the concept under which an intuition produced by practical reason must be subsumed. The pure concept of theoretical reason is the concept of an object as such.[128] An intuition produced by reason under the schema of such a concept, can only be a formal determination of space and time.[129] The faculty whereby reason subsumes the form of intuition under the concept of an object as such, is judgment.[130]

Reason judges the agreement of the form of a sensible intuition with the concept of an object as such. This agreement or disagreement is thought in the object and intuited in the subject, therefore in time, the form of inner sense, as a feeling of pleasure or displeasure, because it is the agreement or disagreement of the object with the will.[131] The feeling is not grounded upon an interest, a concept, a purpose, or an object, for these all pertain to the matter of cognition, whereas judgment contemplates the form alone.[132] Such a judgment is disinterestedly pleasant, indeterminately universal, purposelessly purposive, subjectively necessary.[133] The pleasure is taken through an object, but not a determinate one, therefore an indeterminate one, an object of pure thought.[134] And what is indeterminate theoretically is determined by practical reason.[135] Thus, the objects of practical

---

126 Kant, *Pure Reason*, B193-197.

127 *Pure Reason*, B10-B14, B176-187.

128 *Pure Reason*, B128, A108-110, A248-253; Reich, *Completeness*, 21-29.

129 Kant, *Judgment*, ak. 221-236; *Pure Reason*, B152-157. Because the concept is indeterminate, the intuition must also be indeterminate, i.e. formal, not material; and because the intuition must be produced by the subject, as it affects itself in inner sense.

130 *Judgment*, ak. 176-181, 188-192, 195-198, 286-291, 208'-251'.

131 *Judgment*, ak. 186-198, 205'-208'.

132 *Judgment*, ak. 203-278.

133 *Judgment*, ak. 211, 219, 236, 240.

134 *Judgment*, ak. 337-354.

135 Gress, *Harmony*, 6-14. The concept of an object as such is logical; the transcendental object is theoretical; the concept of a noumenon is a transcendent idea of reason. The transcendental object arises from the concept of an object in general when the latter is applied to intuition. The concept of a thing in itself arises from the concept of an object whose concept and intuition are identical, a concept that is itself to underlie all nature. The transcendental object and the thing in itself are distinguished by Kant in his first Critique. That there should be a thing in itself, underlying the sensible world, is undetermined by theoretical reason. Thus it may appear, that I have substituted the indeterminate

reason—the immortality of the soul, the freedom of the will, and the existence of God—are also objects of theoretical reason, being verified by aesthetic judgment. What is negated of theoretical reason, and infinitely beyond it in practical reason, is affirmed by aesthetic judgment.[136]

A disjunctive judgment consists of mutually grounded particulars under a common universal. The particular judgments are grounds of one another, therefore also of the whole. If, then, there is in God a person thought through the relation of community and reciprocity, this person depends upon both the Father and the Son, who depend upon one another in his procession. Because he depends upon both the Father and the Son, he is a person distinct from the Father and the Son, and one God with the Father and the Son. And because he is the community of the Father and the Son, he is called, the Spirit.

There are therefore only these three divine persons, the Father, the Son, and the Holy Spirit, for the Spirit is the totality of the divine persons, to which there can be no addition.

The legal judgment of the Holy Spirit, through which his person is known, must depend upon the judgments of the Father and the Son. In the judgment of the Spirit, the judgments of negation and infinity are harmonized. Negation and infinity agree in affirmation; therefore, the Spirit's judgment is affirmative. Legal affirmation is justification; therefore, the role of the Spirit is to justify Christ in his submission to unconditional condemnation.

Because the Spirit's justification contains within itself both the condemnation of the Father and the submission of the Son, it is one and the same inward lawfulness by which the Spirit justifies, the Son submits, and the Father condemns, and the Holy Spirit is one God with the Father and the Son.

It is not lawful for a righteous man to be condemned without his consent; therefore, that man must also be justified in giving his consent to

---

concept of a noumenon for that of an object as such, and then claimed determination of it by practical reason. However, the concept of an object as such underlies all concepts of objects, both theoretical and practical, and is identical in every conception of an object. Furthermore, it is by an act of judgment that the indeterminate concept of a noumenon, and the one determined by practical reason, are the same, for although they are both concepts of noumena, they are really united as underlying nature, and this unity is cognized by judgment.

[136] Deut. 30:19; Job 37:1-5; Ps. 8, 19, 29; Rom. 1:18-25.

condemnation. That condemnation is unconditional; therefore, the consent itself is grounded upon the condemnation, and the justification of his consent is grounded upon both together. The moral law requires one person for each judgment executed; therefore, it is lawful for God to condemn a righteous man, because God is a Trinity.

Thus, infinity makes an affirmation of negation. God is the spirit of affirmation, and even negation in God is affirmation.

PART II—THE TRINITY

SECTION 4—THE ESSENCE OF GOD

Definition

A mode is the relation of the concept of an object to the thinking subject, by which the concept refers to an object, whether possible, actual, or necessary.[1]

Explication

All forms of judgment are activities of the thinking subject and are originally conceived in the subject's self-consciousness, which is expressed by the proposition, "I think."[2] Thought is the *universal* activity of a *particular* thinking subject;[3] thought is *affirmed* of the thinking subject, which is distinguished from every other through *negation*. The relation of thought to the thinking subject is the original of *categorical* judgments. The relation of thought to an object is the original form of *hypothetical* judgments.[4] The relation of thought itself to all particular thinking subjects and objects thought is the form of *disjunctive* judgments.

Universality and affirmation are formal principles; particularity and negation are material.[5] The formal and the material combined yield singular and infinite judgments. Singular and infinite judgments are formally

---

[1] Kant, *Pure Reason*, B265-294.

[2] *Pure Reason*, A119, A123-126, B131-142; Reich, *Completeness*, 21-39. This is thesis of Reich's work, *The Completeness of Kant's Table of Judgments*. The direct derivation of the categories from the unity of apperception, *I think*, is mine. Kant never demonstrated the completeness of his table of categories, nor derived the forms of judgment from the power of thought (*Pure Reason* Axvi-xvii, B108-109). I am indebted to Klaus Reich for introducing me to the solution of this problem.

[3] Reich, *Completeness*, 34. And therefore the same forms of thought belong to all rational beings, and by the same argument, the moral law is valid for all.

[4] Kant, *Logic*, Section 24-25. In the form of hypothetical judgments, thought is not cognized as the subject, and the object as its predicate, because thought is itself predicated of the thinking subject. Thought is a representation that mediates between the object and the thinking subject. The form of hypothetical judgments is therefore distinct from that of categorical judgments.

[5] *Pure Reason*, B33-35, B118; *Logic*, Section 2, 18; Aristotle, *Metaphysics* 1032a33-1032b1, 1033a8-11, 1033b20-22, 1034a5-8.

identical to universal and affirmative ones, materially identical to particulars and negatives.[6]

Universality and particularity, and also affirmation and negation, are distinct in thought; wherefore, their identity belongs not to thought, but to intuition, and by the singular and the infinite, intuition is defined. An intuition is a universal that contains within itself its own particularity, an affirmation of that which is other than thought.[7]

Sensible intuition distinguishes the singular from the universal, and the infinite from the affirmative. Therefore, sensible intuition is distinct from thought, and must itself be subsumed under concepts, to be thought by the thinking subject. This subsumption takes place through the forms of judgment, through which all thoughts are thought by the thinking subject.[8] Hence, the activity of the thinking subject determines the form of experience, while the object determines its matter.[9] The logical forms of judgment applied to intuition are called *categories*.[10]

All subsumption takes place through a common element. Because concepts and intuitions are distinct, the common element is not contained in either, but in their combination. This is both concept and intuition, the concept of intuitions, and the intuition of concepts.[11] An intuition as such is not a concept, but their combination is, and may therefore be subsumed under concepts, and may also subsume intuitions under itself.

Concepts and intuitions both belong to the thinking subject, as its representations.[12] Their synthesis is a work of the subject, through which it intuits itself and its thought. The concept of such an intuition is time, the form of inner sense. In time, concepts are intuited, and intuitions are conceived. This is the imaginative synthesis, through which all empirical knowledge is possible.[13]

Concepts are prior to intuitions; therefore, the categories apply to intuition a priori.[14] All concepts, even empirical concepts, if thinkable not as aggregates of particulars, but as strict universals, are explicated through the

---

[6] Kant, *Pure Reason*, B96-98; *Logic*, Section 21-22.
[7] *Pure Reason*, B33, B96-98.
[8] *Pure Reason*, B104-105; Reich, *Completeness*, 1-19.
[9] Kant, *Pure Reason*, B1-2, B33-34, B74-76, A124-125, A128, B150-152.
[10] *Pure Reason*, B104-105, A119, B143.
[11] *Pure Reason*, B74-76, A98-128, B150-165.
[12] *Pure Reason*, B33-34, B74-76, A98-99, A103-110, B131-143.
[13] *Pure Reason*, A98-110, B150-156, B176-187.
[14] *Pure Reason*, B163-165.

categories.[15] Therefore, natural beauties and natural purposes, such as plants and animals, which are truly empirical concepts, nevertheless accord with the rules of the understanding, because their aesthetic reveals the concept of a supersensible object.[16] Thus, plants and animals are immutable purposes of nature, which reproduce according to their kinds, and with all others form a community of living things, itself an end of nature.[17]

The thinking subject conceives of an object as that to which thought is particular, and which is universal to thought. As universal concept, it is explicated through the functions of thought. Because it possesses quantity, it also possesses quality, relation, and lastly, modality.

Thought refers to objects mediately or immediately.[18] The particular contains the universal, and particular concepts refer to objects, for in the particular, the universal is itself that to which thought is particular. However, concepts distinguish the particular from the universal, and thus the object to which the particular refers. Therefore, mere concepts refer to objects indirectly, through the mediation of particulars.

Intuition contains the identity of the universal with the particular. As the particular contains the universal, so also the universal contains the particular. It follows that intuition refers immediately to objects, because an intuition contains within itself the concept of the object to which its particular refers.

The particular is the distinguishing condition of the universal; the universal may only be regarded as particular through the particular.[19] For every distinction there is a distinguishing condition, but because mere concepts do not possess within themselves their particularity, the objects to which they refer are indeterminate. A concept may be either subject or predicate, and one categorical judgment may be either ground or consequent, etc. The condition and the conditioned as such are always determined, but which concept is condition or conditioned is not determined, and may be converted according to the rules of logic.

Intuitions, however, refer directly to objects, and contain their distinguishing conditions within themselves. Therefore, the categories determine

---

[15] Kant, *Pure Reason*, B165. The universal is the first; all others follow with it.

[16] *Judgment*, ak. 193, 246, 410-415.

[17] *Judgment*, ak. 357-429, esp. Section 64.

[18] *Pure Reason*, B33, B92-94.

[19] *Pure Reason*, B92-94, B455; Reich, *Completeness*, 34-37; Aristotle, *Metaphysics* 1033b19-26, 1034a5-8.

intuitions according to the functions of thought. Substance is that which is always subject, never predicate; cause is that which is always ground, never consequent, and etc.[20]

The universal is particularized in the singular. Sensible intuition distinguishes the universal from the singular; therefore, the sensible understanding cannot refer its concepts directly to objects. Objects of intellectual intuition, or things in themselves, the sensible understanding may think, but not know.[21]

Concepts refer to objects, and to themselves; therefore, objects refer also to concepts, and the thinking subject is conscious of itself through objects. Consciousness and the self are distinct, as universal to particular. They are identified in self-consciousness, for the self is conscious of itself as the conscious self. Self-consciousness is singular, and refers to the concept of an object, through which the subject is conscious of itself.

If, then, the subject conceives of itself, it conceives also of objects to which its concepts refer, which refer also to them. And as there are concepts that think the reference of concepts to an object, so also there are concepts that think the reciprocal reference of objects to concepts. These concepts are called the *modalities*.[22]

The modalities think the agreement of the concept of the object with the object itself, through concepts of the reference of an object to the subject. The object is first conceived by the subject through the relations. The modalities then conceive the thinking subject through the object. They think the matter of an object, formally conceived through the relations, without adding to its concept, but only the relation of the object to the thinking faculty.[23] As the matter of an object opposes its form, the modalities are inversions of the relations, as qualities are of quantities.[24] They

---

[20] Kant, *Pure Reason*, B128-129.

[21] This limitation is upon the human race; angels are not bound by it, because they do not distinguish between concepts and intuitions. They do indeed distinguish between the universal and the particular, but since they identify the universal and the singular, for them, universal concepts already refer to objects. Although they identify them, yet because they distinguish the universal and the particular, they may conceive the singular through the particular, and so regard the singular as distinct from the universal, distinguishing them in spite of this identification, or rather by virtue of it. Their understanding is superior to ours, because equal to ours and something more, containing the distinction that we make, but also the identity that they alone think.

[22] *Pure Reason*, B99-101, B265-294; Reich, *Completeness*, 54-56, 83-87, 103.

[23] Kant, *Pure Reason*, B99-101, B266; *Logic*, Section 30.

[24] Reich, *Completeness*, 83-87.

think the agreement of condition with conditioned by thinking the conditioned as condition of the condition. In the object, the condition and its conditioned are exchanged for one another. The exchange is itself the test whereby the understanding judges whether and how its concepts refer to objects.

The modalities are therefore marvelous concepts, through which the concept of an object is given objective validity through mere concepts of the thinking subject.

The singular is the concept of an object. The identity of the self and its consciousness is singular, and contains the form of an object. The thinking subject thinks itself through thought; therefore, thought is the undetermined object of the thinking subject. The concept of an object that contains the self's mere consciousness is *problematic*.[25]

Through consciousness of itself, the subject conceives of that to which thought is particular. The concept of such an object is therefore determinate, that is, particular and distinct, the matter with the form. Through consciousness of determinate objects, the thinking subject is conscious of itself. The self determines its own consciousness, as the one that thinks a determinate object. It is a particular self, distinct from thought in general, and from all other thinking subjects. The concept of an object that contains the subject's self-consciousness is *assertoric*.[26]

Self-consciousness is consciousness of the self, as the self of which it is conscious. Thus, the thinking subject conceives of an object that is determinate through its concept, and assertoric by virtue of its problem. The concept of an object that contains the subject's self-consciousness within consciousness of the self is *apodictic*.[27]

The problematic judgment refers to the agreement between subject and predicate in a categorical judgment; the assertoric, to the agreement between ground and consequent in a hypothetical; the apodictic, to the agreement between whole and part in a disjunctive. The agreement is thought through the representation of the predicate as condition of the subject, the consequent as condition of the ground, or the part as condition of the whole. In the relations, the conditioned must agree with and be

---

[25] Kant, *Pure Reason*, B99-101; *Logic*, Section 30. An object of a problematic judgment is thinkable. This is indicated by the word *may*. Questions are also problematic judgments.

[26] *Pure Reason*, B99-101; *Logic*, Section 30.

[27] *Pure Reason*, B99-101; *Logic*, Section 30.

subsumed under its condition. In the modalities, then, the condition must rather agree with, and be subsumed under the conditioned.

All subsumption takes place through a common element. There must therefore belong to the conditioned that which explicates its fitness to be the conditioned of the condition, whether as predicate of the subject, consequent of the ground, or part of the whole.

In pure general logic, concepts refer to other concepts as the objects with which they must agree.[28] To refer the logical forms of judgment to real objects, rather than logical ones, intuition is required. When an intuition is given, it is subsumed under the forms of judgment. The categories of modality are *possibility, actuality,* and *necessity.*[29]

Possibility does not follow from the problematic,[30] neither actuality from the assertoric,[31] nor necessity from the apodictic.[32] Although they employ the same function of thought, they differ in application; the latter apply to concepts, the former to intuitions. What is logically possible is thinkable; its concept is coherent, non-contradictory, but this is far from a coherent intuition, which requires agreement with the formal conditions of experience.[33] What is logically possible, or problematic, is therefore not necessarily possible in reality.

With the modalities, the tables of judgments and of categories are complete. The judgments and categories are divided into two classes: concepts, and relations of concepts.[34] Each class divides concepts into formal and material principles of the understanding. Each heading is divided into three moments, save that in pure general logic the third moments of quantity and of quality are omitted. This yields ten logical forms of judgment and twelve categories.[35]

This is the demonstration of the completeness of the tables of judgments and of categories.[36] The forms of judgment apply to the form of the

---

[28] Kant, *Pure Reason*, B79, 83-85, B128-129, A103-105, A108-110, B137, B140-142, A248-253; Reich 28-29, 65-67, 87-92.

[29] Kant, *Pure Reason*, B106.

[30] *Pure Reason*, B267-268.

[31] *Pure Reason*, B272-273.

[32] *Pure Reason*, B279.

[33] *Pure Reason*, B265, B267-272.

[34] *Pure Reason*, B110, B220-223, B692; *Practical Reason*, 5:103-104; *Prolegomena*, Section 39, footnote 19.

[35] *Pure Reason*, B95-98, B106.

[36] Reich, *Completeness*, 101-109.

understanding, the agreement of thought with itself; therefore, in them nothing is thought but the form of a concept. The form of a concept is its reference to another concept, and the reference itself is a concept; therefore, the tables divide concepts from their relations. The concepts of the first class are absolute; those of the second are relative.[37] This is a division according to concepts, because the classes are concepts under which the functions of thought are classified. Division according to concepts is two-fold, to be proven below. It follows that the division of classes is twofold: concepts, and relations of concepts.

The classes think the form of concepts. The form of concepts refers to the matter of concepts, and the matter of concepts, thought through the form, is itself a form and function of thought. Therefore, each class is divided into two headings, one for thinking the form of concepts, and another for thinking their matter. The material concepts are opposites of the formal. Quantity thinks the particular through the universal, whereas quality thinks the universal through the particular. Likewise, relation thinks the conditioned through the condition, whereas modality thinks the condition through its conditioned. This is a division according to concepts and is also twofold. The four headings are therefore: quantity, quality, relation, and modality.[38]

The headings are concepts according to which the functions of thought are classified. Every heading must therefore contain within itself several concepts classified by the heading. A concept contains within itself a reference to another concept; hence, division according to relation is threefold: referrer, referent, and reference. Each heading is itself a concept and contains these three moments in order. However, division according to concepts excludes reference and is therefore twofold. For this reason, the categories include the moments of reference in quantity and quality, but the forms of judgment exclude them.[39]

The categories are concepts for thinking the application of concepts to objects. They include concepts for thinking intuition, because intuition makes possible the transition from concepts to objects.[40] However, the judgments contemplate only the form of thought, not its employment; in them therefore all the reference of pure concepts is excluded. Each of these

---

[37] Kant, *Pure Reason*, B110; *Prolegomena*, Section 39 footnote; Reich, *Completeness*, 87-92.
[38] Kant, *Pure Reason*, B95, B106.
[39] Reich, *Completeness*, 105-109.
[40] Kant, *Pure Reason*, B96-98; Reich, *Completeness*, 105-109.

moments is formally identical to the first, but materially distinct. Consequently, the reckoning of fundamental concepts according to their form excludes them as distinct concepts, but their reckoning according to matter includes them. There are therefore ten logical forms of judgment and twelve categories.

There are, accordingly, ten commandments, for morality is as logic itself; and there are twelve sons of Jacob, and twelve apostles, for doctrines are as things; whereof the numbers are named in and by the word of God, according to the λογος of things.[41] And the natural beauties and purposes of the world are divided by the categories in the days of creation, six of work, one of rest, for the formal categories are united with the material in the aesthetic representation of a supersensible object, and the completeness of the whole is distinct from them all, because each one is distinguished from the others in time.[42]

The order of fundamental concepts is determined by this rule: that through which another is thought is prior, and that which is thought through another is posterior.[43]

A faculty is the thinking subject thought of as condition of the concept of an object.[44] Objects are either problematic, assertoric, or apodictic, and there are three faculties, understanding, reason, and judgment.[45] The understanding is the subjective condition for a problematic judgment, whereby no object is thought but that which may be given through intuition. Reason is the subjective condition of an assertoric judgment, whereby the intuition of an object is produced through the activity of the thinking subject. Judgment is the subjective condition of an apodictic judgment, whereby the thinking subject gives to itself the intuition of an object. The thinking subject is therefore the ground of concepts, intuitions, and the identity of concepts and intuitions.

The persons are divine particulars; in them the divine nature inheres. To validate the concepts of the persons, that is, to refer them to the divine nature, as subsisting therein, requires concepts for thinking the nature as condition of the persons, each person being thought distinctly within the

---

[41] Gen. 35:22, 42:13, 32, 49:28; Ex. 28:21, 34:28, 39:14, etc.; Deut. 4:13, 10:4; Matt. 10:1, 11:1, 20:17; Luke 6:13, 9:1, 22:14; Acts 6:2; Rev. 21:14; John 1:1-5.
[42] Gen. 1:5, 8, 13, 19, 23, 31, 2:2-3.
[43] Kant, *Pure Reason*, B89-92.
[44] *Groundwork*, 4:412-413; *Judgment*, ak. 172, 220.
[45] *Judgment*, ak. 198, 246'.

unity of the nature. The modalities are the required concepts; without them, the application of the concept *person* to God is indeed valid subjectively, but not objectively. Through the modalities, the persons are understood as belonging to the divine nature itself, and not merely to our conception of it.

The modalities are relations of the divine nature to the thinking faculty. The divine persons are known through the modalities. The nature of God is thought according to its concept, its intuition, and the identity of its concept and its intuition, for God is holy, and holiness is the identity of righteousness and blessedness. The Father is the concept of God, or his righteousness; the Son is the intuition of God, or his blessedness; and the Spirit is the identity of concept and intuition in God, or his holiness.

There is, for each divine person, a mode through which he is known, but the divine persons are known through their judgments upon Jesus Christ, because the judgments are lawful for the sake of the persons judging. Thus, the modalities are conditions of the lawfulness of the judgments. Each judgment is thought through a modality, and the person revealed in the judgment is known according to the modality thought. The Father's condemnation is possible, the Son's nonlegal righteousness is actual, and the Spirit's justification is necessary.

The modalities restrict the knowledge of each person to a distinct faculty, and through these restrictions make possible the knowledge of distinct persons,[46] for the faculties are one and the same reason operating according to different modes, whereby the mind is well-fitted to receive the knowledge of one God in three persons.[47]

Proposition 1

The Father's condemnation is possible.

Proof

The Father is God unconditionally, and his condemnation is unconditional. What is unconditional negates any condition under which it may be

---

[46] Kant, *Pure Reason*, B265-267. It is by limiting the understanding that it achieves certainty in its domain.

[47] Augustine, *Trinity* Books 8-15; Aquinas, *Summa* 1.27.1-5.

given to us in experience, for what is given to us in experience is given through its agreement with a prior condition. Thus, the Father's condemnation is thought through a concept, without intuition. The concept of the divine nature is righteousness, and what is righteous is morally possible. Therefore, the Father is the righteousness of God, and his condemnation is possible.

Scripture Proof

> O my Father, if it be possible, let this cup pass from me; nevertheless not as I will, but as thou *wilt*. Matthew 26:39, cf. Mark 14:36, Luke 22:42, John 10:17-18

> Yet it pleased the LORD to bruise him. Isaiah 53:11, cf. Col. 1:19-20

By God's pleasure, I understand mere agreement with the moral law.

> My God, my God, why hast thou forsaken me? Psalm 22:1

A question is a problematic judgment. What is problematic, is logically possible, and morality is as logic itself. Therefore, this question refers to the possibility of the Father's condemnation. *My God, my God*, God, the Father. He is therefore the righteousness of God.

> Of righteousness, because I go to my Father, and ye see me no more. John 16:10

> O righteous Father, the world hath not known thee: but I have known thee, and these have known that thou hast sent me. John 17:25

> And if any man sin, we have an advocate with the Father, Jesus Christ the righteous: And he is the propitiation for our sins: and not for ours only, but also for *the sins of* the whole world. 1 John 2:1-2

Then shall the righteous shine forth as the sun in the kingdom of their Father. Who hath ears to hear, let him hear. Matthew 13:43

Power is in a peculiar manner attributed to the Father.

Therefore doth my Father love me, because I lay down my life, that I might take it again. No man taketh it from me, but I lay it down of myself. I have power to lay it down, and I have power to take it again. This commandment have I received of my Father. John 10:17-18

My Father, which gave *them* me, is greater than all; and no *man* is able to pluck *them* out of my Father's hand. John 10:29

Father, the hour is come, glorify thy Son, that thy Son also may glorify thee: As thou hast given him power over all flesh, that he should give eternal life to as many as thou hast given him. And this is life eternal, that they might know thee the only true God, and Jesus Christ, whom thou hast sent. John 17:1-3

See also Ex. 13:5, 11-12; Num. 14:23; Deut. 1:8, 35, 4:30-31, 6:10-12, &etc.; 2 Chron. 14:4; Jer. 11:4; Matt. 3:9, 26:53; John 5:19, 30; Luke 3:8; Rom. 4:11.

Comment

Concepts inhere in the thinking subject.[48] The concept of an object is thought through the relation of a concept to an object, and is validated through the reciprocal relation of the object to the concept. Thus, an object is formally conceived through the relation of one concept to another. This relation is that of predicate to subject in a categorical judgment, and the object thought through the agreement of the subject with the predicate is problematic.

A substance is that which fills a space in time. The agreement between the perception of a substance and the substance perceived is the form of an object, through which experience is possible, for what is problematic in

---

[48] Kant, *Pure Reason*, B131-136, B403-404, A348-351, B407.

concepts is possible in things. The question is, does the perception agree or disagree, in its concept and its intuition, with the underlying subject? If they agree, the perception is said to be possible.[49]

The possibility of forming a sphere out of a given matter depends upon whether the form of the sphere agrees with the matter of substance. A substance fills a space in time, and a sphere is a determination of space. The form agrees with the matter, and the experience is possible. On the other hand, the impossibility of a point substance appears from the disagreement of the predicate with the underlying subject, for a substance fills a space, while a point is not the filling of a space, but a boundary.[50]

The paralogisms of pure reason think perceptions as accidents inhering in the thinking subject. This inference is problematic, and under the supposition that the objects of sense are things in themselves, the conclusion is possible. Concepts inhere in the thinking subject; therefore, intuitions identified with concepts may be thought of as inhering in the thinking subject, though reason may also think the subject as a property of its intuitions, and pure reason is without any condition under which it may know either of these possibilities to be actual.

Practical reason presupposes the possibility of man's final end. This possibility is the basis for aesthetic judgment, for in every such judgment, reason takes pleasure in the agreement of the form of an object with the concept of an object as such; that is, the natural world is seen in agreement with the end prescribed by practical reason, and this end is understood to be possible.

How does the person of the Father agree with the divine nature? The Father is God unconditionally; the agreement of his person with the divine nature is thought through his own person. The divine nature is unconditional in its concept, and the concept of the divine nature is its righteousness; therefore, the Father is the concept of God, or his righteousness.

The Father is known through unconditional condemnation. The condemnation itself is possible, because it agrees in thought with the moral law. A concept that contains the ground of an intuition agrees with the intuition to be produced, and is possible. The condemnation of the Father is possible because he is the righteousness of God. As the manifestation of

---

[49] Kant, *Pure Reason*, B265-272, B286.
[50] *Pure Reason*, B211; *Natural Science*, 87.

the divine nature is a supreme end of the moral law, so is the revelation of the Father subsisting therein, who is an end in himself.

Proposition 2

The Son's nonlegal righteousness is actual.

Proof

The nonlegal righteousness of Christ depends upon the unconditional condemnation of the Father. It is thought upon a prior condition, under which his person may be given in an intuition, for what is thought through a concept is an intuition. Thus, the lawfulness of the Son's submission to condemnation is intuited, and what agrees in intuition with the moral law is actual, or blessed. Therefore, the Son is the blessedness of God, and his nonlegal righteousness is actual.

Scripture Proof

and hath translated *us* into the kingdom of his dear Son: In whom we have redemption through his blood, *even* the forgiveness of sins: Who is the image of the invisible God, the firstborn of all creation. Colossians 1:14-15

Who being the brightness of *his* glory, and the express image of his person, when he had by himself purged our sins, sat down on the right hand of the Majesty on high. Hebrews 1:3

By his shed blood, Jesus Christ reveals the Father to us.

Father, the hour is come; glorify thy Son, that thy Son also may glorify thee. John 17:1-5

Therefore, when he was gone out, Jesus said, Now is the Son of man glorified, and God is glorified in him. John 13:31

The Son shows himself to be the image of God, the intuition of the divine nature, through his submission to condemnation, in dependence on the Father.

> For God so loved the world, that he gave his only begotten Son. John 3:16

> I proceeded forth and came from God; neither came I of myself, but he sent me. John 8:42

Jesus Christ is to be believed and obeyed, because he does not come in his own name, but in the name of the Father who sent him.

> He that speaketh of himself seeketh his own glory: but he that seeketh his glory that sent him, the same is true, and no unrighteousness is in him. John 7:18

> I can of mine own self do nothing: as I hear, I judge: and my judgment is just; because I seek not mine own will, but the will of the Father which hath sent me. If I bear witness of myself, my witness is not true. There is another that beareth witness of me; and I know that the witness which he witnesseth of me is true. Ye sent unto John... But I have greater witness than *that* of John: for the works which the Father hath given me to finish, the same works that I do, bear witness of me, that the Father hath sent me. And the Father himself, which hath sent me, hath borne witness of me. John 5:30-33, 36-37, cf. John 5:19-47, 6:32-40, 8:18-19, 28-29, 50, 10:18

Wherefore, he is the blessedness of God.

> And the multitudes that went before, and that followed, cried, saying, Hosanna to the Son of David: Blessed *is* he that cometh in the name of the Lord; Hosanna in the highest. Matthew 21:9, cf. Mark 14:61, Luke 19:38

> Whose *are* the fathers, and of whom as concerning the flesh Christ *came*, who is over all, God blessed for ever. Amen. Romans 9:5

Blessed *be* God, even the Father of our Lord Jesus Christ, the Father of mercies, and the God of all comfort; Who comforteth us in all our tribulation, that we may be able to comfort them which are in any trouble, by the comfort wherewith we ourselves are comforted of God. For as the sufferings of Christ abound in us, so our consolation also aboundeth by Christ. 2 Corinthians 1:3-5

Blessed *be* the God and Father of our Lord Jesus Christ, who hath blessed us with all spiritual blessings in heavenly *places* in Christ. Ephesians 1:3, cf. 2 Cor. 1:3-5, 11:31, Tit. 2:13, 1 Pet. 1:3

And she spake out with a loud voice, and said, Blessed *art* thou among women, and blessed *is* the fruit of thy womb. Luke 1:42

Kiss the Son, lest he be angry, and ye perish *from* the way, when his wrath is kindled but a little. Blessed *are* all they that put their trust in him. Psalm 2:12

Whereas power is ascribed to the Father, to the Son is attributed the performance of God's will.

My meat is to do the will of him that sent me, and to finish his work. John 4:36

For I came down from heaven, not to do mine own will, but the will of him that sent me. John 6:38

I am the good shepherd, and know my *sheep*, and am known of mine. As the Father knoweth me, even so know I the Father: and I lay down my life for the sheep. And other sheep I have, which are not of this fold: them also I must bring, and they shall hear my voice; and there shall be one fold, *and* one shepherd. Therefore doth my Father love me, because I lay down my life, that I might take it again. No man taketh it from me, but I lay it down of myself. I have power to lay it down, and I have power to take it again. This commandment have I received of my Father. John 10:14-18

And I give unto them eternal life; and they shall never perish, neither shall any *man* pluck them out of my hand. John 10:28

These words spake Jesus, and lifted up his eyes to heaven, and said, Father, the hour is come; glorify thy Son, that thy Son also may glorify thee: As thou hast given him power over all flesh, that he should give eternal life to as many as thou hast given him. And this is life eternal, that they might know thee the only true God, and Jesus Christ, whom thou hast sent. I have glorified thee on the earth: I have finished the work which thou gavest me to do. And now, O Father, glorify thou me with thine own self with the glory which I had with thee before the world was. John 17:1-5

And the actuality of divine righteousness.

And the Word was made flesh, and dwelt among us, (and we beheld his glory, the glory as of the only begotten of the Father,) full of grace and truth. John 1:14, cf. vs. 18, Matt. 11:27, Luke 10:22

And no man hath ascended up to heaven, but he that came down from heaven, *even* the Son of man which is in heaven. John 3:13

Jesus saith unto him, I am the way, the truth, and the life: no man cometh unto the Father, but by me. If ye had known me, ye should have known my Father also: and from henceforth ye know him, and have seen him. Philip saith unto him, Lord, shew us the Father, and it sufficeth us. Jesus saith unto him, Have I been so long time with you, and yet hast thou not known me, Philip? He that hath seen me hath seen the Father; and how sayest thou *then*, Shew us the Father? John 14:6-9

That which was from the beginning, which we have heard, which we have seen with our eyes, which we have looked upon, and our hands have handled, of the Word of life; (For the life was manifested, and we have seen *it*, and bear witness, and shew unto you that eternal life, which was with the Father, and was manifested unto us;) That which we have seen and heard declare we unto you, that ye also may have fellowship with us: and truly our fellowship *is* with the Father, and with his Son Jesus Christ. 1 John 1:1-4

Be not thou therefore ashamed of the testimony of our Lord, nor of me his prisoner: but be thou partaker of the afflictions of the gospel according to the power of God; Who hath saved us, and called *us* with an holy calling, not according to our works, but according to his own purpose and grace, which was given us in Christ Jesus before the world began, But is now made manifest by the appearing of our Saviour Jesus Christ, who hath abolished death, and hath brought life and immortality to light through the gospel. 2 Timothy 1:8-10

Therefore, he says to his disciples,

But blessed *are* your eyes, for they see: and your ears, for they hear. For verily I say unto you, That many prophets and righteous *men* have desired to see *those things* which ye see, and have not seen *them*; and to hear *those things* which ye hear, and have not heard *them*. Matthew 13:16-17, cf. Luke 10:23-24. Also see Matt. 16:16-17

See also Eph. 1:17-18; 2 Cor. 4:6; Gen. 24:48, 25:11, 27:27; Judg. 13:24, 17:2; 1 Sam. 26:25; 1 Kings 5:7; 2 Chron. 2:12.

Comment

A judgment is assertoric if it agrees with another judgment as its object. Originally, this object is another categorical judgment. Hence, in pure logic, an assertoric judgment is conceived through a hypothetical. In the proposition, "If Socrates is a man, then Socrates is mortal," the latter agrees with the former as its object; the connection itself is assertoric, and the consequent is assertoric upon condition of the antecedent. Although the antecedent may also be assertoric upon a prior judgment, logic refers only to the antecedent as such, not as consequent of another.[51]

The subject is the mediating concept of a categorical judgment; it is also the condition of the judgment itself. Thus, the relation of a categorical

---

[51] Kant, *Pure Reason*, B99-101; *Logic*, Section 30; Reich, *Completeness*, 75-87.

judgment is internal, and the object is formally conceived.[52] The mediating judgment of a hypothetical is neither condition nor conditioned of the hypothetical, but another besides, and the mediating judgment is in agreement with the concept. Thus, the hypothetical relation is external, and conceives the matter of an object with its form.[53]

Determinate objects are thought through the hypothetical relation. The matter of sensation is intuited through causes and effects. The present is grounded in the past, the future in the present; the state of things is caused by the prior state of things, and is the cause of the posterior. Through causality, substance is actual, intuited not only as to its form, but also its matter, because it is through the matter of substance that the prior state determines the posterior.[54]

The antinomies of pure reason are subsumed under the category of actuality. Every conditioned is determined by its condition, and one intuition is given through its relation to another. However, if appearances are things in themselves, then intuitions relate as concepts, and every condition is given not only in connection with the conditioned, but in the conditioned itself, as one concept contains another. Reason then asserts either an unconditioned condition, or an infinite series of conditions, and this not as possible only, but also as actual.[55]

The formal purposiveness of nature yields the matter of an object thought through the form.[56] Whereas aesthetic judgment thinks the form of the world in harmony with moral purposes, teleological judgment sees the matter of the world in agreement with the same.[57] The world is full of natural purposes, wherein each part exists for the sake of the whole, and the whole for the sake of the part.[58]

The Son submits to condemnation through nonlegal righteousness. His nonlegal righteousness is actual, because it is an intuition produced according to the concept. The Son is glorified in his obedience unto the cursed death of the cross, for if a man cannot be righteous, unless he is to be blessed in his obedience, and Jesus Christ is righteous under the curse,

---

[52] Kant, *Pure Reason*, B265-272; B321-324.

[53] *Pure Reason*, B272-274, B286, B321-324.

[54] *Natural Science*, 75-92; *Opus Postumum*, 21:403, 21:408-409, 22:206.

[55] *Pure Reason*, B518-535.

[56] *Judgment*, ak. 376-384.

[57] *Judgment*, ak. 359-369.

[58] *Judgment*, ak. 369-376.

then Christ's righteousness and blessedness are identical. However, his righteousness is revealed in his obedience, and obedience is not an act of the divine nature. Therefore, the Son is the intuition of God, and subsists in the divine nature, as its blessedness.

Proposition 3

The Holy Spirit's justification is necessary.

Proof

God justifies the righteous, therefore God justifies Christ. Christ's righteousness consists of his submission to condemnation. His justification is mutually dependent on both the Father's condemnation and the Son's nonlegal righteousness. Thus, the justification of the Holy Spirit is thought through an intuition, or intuited in a concept, that is, in feeling or inner sense. The lawfulness of the Spirit's justification is felt, and what agrees in feeling with the moral law is necessary and holy. Therefore, the Spirit is the holiness of God, and his justification is necessary.

Scripture Proof

The Spirit's justification is necessary according to the rule, that God justifies the righteous.

> Then hear thou in heaven, and do, and judge thy servants, condemning the wicked, to bring his way upon his head; and justifying the righteous, to give him according to his righteousness. 1 Kings 8:32, see also Ex. 23:7, 2 Chron. 6:23

The Spirit's justification is necessary, because through it Christ offers himself to God, and through it also God receives the sacrifice of his Son.

> How much more shall the blood of Christ, who through the eternal Spirit offered himself without spot to God, purge your conscience from dead works to serve the living God? Hebrews 9:14

Scripture joins the justification of the Spirit to feeling, for the Spirit is the breath of God.

> And walk in love, as Christ also hath loved us, and hath given himself for us an offering and a sacrifice to God for a sweet smelling savour. Ephesians 5:2, cf. Gen. 8:20-21, Lev. 1:9, 13, 17, &etc., see also Gen. 1:1-3 and Ps. 33:6

> The pleasure of the LORD shall prosper in his hand. Isaiah 53:10

The Spirit is called holy, because he is the holiness of God, "the spirit of holiness" (Romans 1:4).

> That thy beloved may be delivered: save *with* thy right hand, and answer me. God hath spoken in his holiness... Psalm 108:6-7

> For there are three that bear record in heaven, the Father, the Word, and the Holy Ghost: and these three are one. And there are three that bear witness in earth, the spirit, and the water, and the blood: and these three agree in one. 1 John 5:7-8

The spirit refers to the justification of the Spirit; *the water* to the fleshly submission of Christ; *the blood* to the condemnation of the Father (cf. Matt. 26:39-41). The judgments of the persons bear record in earth to the persons, who bear record in heaven. The justification of the Spirit is necessary, because it is referred to by the name of the justifier.

Necessity is ascribed to the Holy Ghost through the unity of the Father and the Son in the divine nature, for if power belongs to the Father, and action to the Son, then to the Holy Spirit belongs necessity.

> And I give unto them eternal life; and they shall never perish, neither shall any *man* pluck them out of my hand. My Father, which gave *them* me, is greater than all; and no *man* is able to pluck *them* out of my Father's hand. I and *my* Father are one. John 10:28-30

Wherefore, the truth of the Gospel follows from the saying of it.

And Pilate asked him, saying, Art thou the King of the Jews? And he answered him and said, Thou sayest *it*. Luke 23:3

Then Pilate entered into the judgment hall again, and called Jesus, and said unto him, Art thou the King of the Jews? Jesus answered him, Sayest thou this thing of thyself, or did others tell it thee of me? Pilate answered, Am I a Jew? Thine own nation and the chief priests have delivered thee unto me: what hast thou done? Jesus answered, My kingdom is not of this world: if my kingdom were of this world, then would my servants fight, that I should not be delivered to the Jews: but now is my kingdom not from hence. Pilate therefore said unto him, Art thou a king then? Jesus answered, Thou sayest that I am a king. To this end was I born, and for this cause came I into the world, that I should bear witness unto the truth. Every one that is of the truth heareth my voice. Pilate saith unto him, What is truth? And when he had said this, he went out again unto the Jews, and saith unto them, I find in him no fault *at all*. John 18:33-40

For the "Spirit of truth" gives voice to the truth (John 16:13).

See also Matt. 1:16; Acts 4:12.

Comment

An apodictic judgment is assertoric through its problem.[59] The agreement of the judgment with its object is thought through concepts, by the mutual exclusion of particulars in a disjunctive judgment.[60] One or the other particular refers to the object, because of the universal concept under which they stand.[61]

The universal is the objective ground of the mutual exclusion of particulars in a disjunctive judgment. God, as thought itself, is the objective ground of particular thinking subjects and of objects thought. Therefore, thought itself, the universal, is the object referred to, and the subject is

---

[59] Kant, *Pure Reason*, B99-101; Reich, *Completeness*, 55-56.
[60] Kant, *Pure Reason*, B98-101; Reich, *Completeness*, 83-87.
[61] Kant, *Logic*, Section 29. A color must be either red, or blue, or etc.

conscious of itself through this object. This is the original of *apodictic* judgments. An *apodictic* judgment is the synthesis of the first two moments of modality; it is assertoric by itself, through its problem. Nothing more is required for God to be an object for me, than for me to think of him, for as he is universal thought itself, thought is the mode proper to him.

The concept of God is the original of disjunctive judgments; such judgments are modeled after him, and without the concept of such a being, there would be no disjunctive judgments, and therefore no self-consciousness in the consciousness of an object. Nevertheless, the existence of God is not proven thereby, only the objectivity of his concept. His concept, of itself, refers to an object, that is, an object of thought.

The mutual determination of substances is necessary; particular substances are included in a single intuition, and exclude one another as parts. Nothing whose parts exclude one another can be single, unless those parts mutually determine one another. Each one must contain within itself a representation of all the others, that the thinking subject may proceed from any one to any other.[62] Reciprocal causality is a consequence of the nature of substance, and its unity as a unity of the parts of an intuition. It is actual through its possibility, or necessary.[63]

The ideal of pure reason is thought of as necessary. If the supposition is granted, that appearances are things in themselves, then there must be a supreme being who contains within himself the ground of all that is, because the concept of such a being is identical to his intuition. Therefore, through the concept of God there is an intuition in agreement therewith: he exists, and his existence is necessary.[64]

The forms of nature and its material purposes are united in man, who is made in the image of God. Man contains within himself the highest purpose of nature, and bears dominion over all creation.[65] This dominion is necessary, according as the material purposes of nature must be brought into harmony with its formal purposiveness, which reveals the possibility of man's final end.[66]

The justification of the Holy Spirit is necessary, because through it the judgments of the Father and the Son are harmonized, for these judgments

---

[62] Kant, *Pure Reason*, B258-259.
[63] *Pure Reason*, B256-265, B279-282, B286-287.
[64] *Pure Reason*, B611-618.
[65] Gen. 1:26-28.
[66] *Judgment*, ak. 231-236.

oppose each other in one divine nature. The divine nature is the identity of righteousness and blessedness, but these are distinguished in the Father and the Son. The person of the Holy Spirit is necessary to think the unity of the divine nature in distinct persons, and his justification is necessary to show forth the divine unity in the diverse judgments executed upon Christ; for so he is called by the attributes of God, and where the Father and the Son are, there also is the Holy Spirit.[67]

> Let him kiss me with the kisses of his mouth: for thy love *is* better than wine. Because of the savour of thy good ointments, thy name *is as* ointment poured forth, therefore do the virgins love thee. Song of Solomon 1:2-3

Let him, Christ, *kiss me*, the church, *with the kisses of his mouth, for thy love*, the Father's, *is better than wine. Because of the savour of thy good ointments*, the Holy Spirit proceeding from the Father and the Son, *thy name is as ointment poured forth*, the Incarnate Son, revealing the Father, revealed by the Holy Spirit, *therefore do the virgins love thee.*

> And straightway coming up out of the water, he saw the heavens opened, and the Spirit like a dove descending upon him: And there came a voice from heaven, *saying*, Thou art my beloved Son, in whom I am well pleased. Mark 1:10-11, cf. Matthew 3:16-17, Luke 3:21-22

He saw the heavens, as the divine nature itself, *opened,* σχιζομενους, divided, schismed, *and the Spirit like a dove descending upon him: And there came a voice from heaven, saying, Thou art my beloved Son, in whom I am well pleased.*

The Spirit is the community and reciprocity of the Godhead. The community and reciprocity of concept and intuition is their identity, and concept and intuition are identified in inner sense, in feeling, whereby the Spirit, who is the holiness of God, is known.

The Father condemns the Son, because the Father is the righteousness of God, for the curse is contrary to the blessing, and the Father is righteous in bestowing the curse upon his Son. The Son submits himself to condemnation, because he is the blessedness of God, for obedience is not divine,

---

[67] Ps. 57:1-3; Heb. 2:9; John 10:27-30, 13:31-17:26; 2 Cor. 13:14; Eph. 4:3; 1 John; 2 John.

and Christ is blessed in his obedience unto the cursed death of the cross. The Spirit justifies Christ in his submission to condemnation, because he is the holiness of God, for justification is the ground of divine blessing, and the blessing of Christ is in his obedience to the Father.

General Comment

The law of non-contradiction states, *positively*, that no predicate contradicts its subject; *negatively*, that one subject is not identical to another.[68]

The doctrine of the Incarnation is, the Son of God is both God and man. Neither the divine nature, nor the human nature, contradict the person of the Son, nor does the unity of his person contradict itself, for the Son is distinguished by the relation of dependence, and he is both God and man in dependence on the Father. Therefore, *positively*, neither the human nor the divine nature contradict his person; *negatively*, neither the human nor the divine nature distinguish his person from itself, and there is no contradiction in doctrine of the Incarnation.

The doctrine of the Trinity is, three persons are one God. The divine nature does not contradict any of the persons. The divine nature does not contradict the person of the Father, because the divine nature belongs to the Father categorically, or independently, as the divine nature itself. The divine nature does not contradict the person of the Son, because the divine nature belongs to the Son in dependence on the Father, for he is God unconditionally, upon a condition.[69] Likewise, the divine nature does not contradict the person of the Holy Spirit, because the divine nature belongs to the Holy Spirit in dependence on both the Father and the Son, who depend upon one another in his procession. Nor are distinct persons identified with one another, because each person is distinguished from the others by the way in which he possesses the divine nature, the Father independently, the Son dependently, the Spirit interdependently. Therefore, *positively*, no subject possesses a contradictory predicate; *negatively*, the common predicate does not identify distinct subjects. There is therefore no contradiction in the doctrine of the Trinity.

---

[68] Kant, *Pure Reason*, B189-193.
[69] John 5:26; *Pure Reason*, B43.

God is an inwardly lawful being. An inwardly lawful being is one whose righteousness and blessedness are identical. This identity is holiness. God is therefore righteous, blessed, and holy.

Concepts are unconditional. The unconditional condemnation of the Father contains within itself the concept of the divine nature in the person of the Father. The concept of the divine nature is righteousness, and the Father is the righteousness of God.

Intuitions are conditional. The nonlegal righteousness of the Son contains within itself the intuition of the divine nature in the person of the Son. The intuition of the divine nature is blessedness, and the Son is the blessedness of God.

The identity of concepts and intuitions is mutually conditional. The mutually conditional justification of the Holy Spirit contains within itself the identity of the concept of God and the intuition of God in the person of the Holy Spirit. The identity of the concept of God and his intuition is holiness, and the Spirit is the holiness of God.

In the divine nature, righteousness and blessedness are identical; their identity is holiness. Therefore, the Father, who is the righteousness of God, is blessed and holy; the Son, who is the blessedness of God, is righteous and holy; and the Spirit, who is the holiness of God, is righteous and blessed.

The Father, the Son, and the Holy Spirit are three persons, one God. The righteousness and blessedness of God are distinguished in the Father and the Son, and identified in the Holy Spirit. Therefore, the distinction of concept and intuition in God is identical to their identity, for the identity thought in the Holy Spirit contains also their distinction thought in the Father and the Son, in distinction therefrom. God is therefore absolutely one.

If God is triune, he is one; and if he is one, then he is triune, for if he is absolutely one, his concept is identical in distinction to his intuition, and contains within itself a reference to a particular divine person. This is the Father. Likewise, the intuition of God is identical to his concept, and in distinction from it, refers to another divine person, the Son. And their identity refers to a third person, the Holy Spirit.

God is three because he is one, and one because he is three. He is three persons, one God, for the divine nature is the predicate, the universal, and is identical to its intuition; it is distinct therefrom through the particular, and the particular's distinction from the universal; and the particular is the concept of a divine person. Therefore, there are three distinct persons in one identical nature.

Because he is three in one, he necessarily exists. His concept is that of a being whose concept is identical in distinction to his intuition. This conception of God is valid for us, because we distinguish intuitions from concepts; it is valid for God, because his intuition is identified with his concept; it is valid for the persons, because these are distinguished; and it is valid in itself, without contradiction, because the identity thought in the Holy Spirit is distinct from the distinction thought in the Father and the Son. There is therefore an intuition in agreement with the concept, being contained within it. God is self-existent; he exists through his concept, as trinity; he exists because he is a trinity.[70]

And because he is a trinity, three subjects of one predicate, he is God. The concept of a trinity contains within itself its intuition, in distinction therefrom; therefore, the concept contains within itself the ground of the intuition, in identity therewith. A concept that contains within itself the ground of its intuition, is righteousness; the intuition in agreement with the concept, blessedness; and their identity, holiness. The Trinity is therefore righteous, blessed, and holy, an inwardly lawful being. Therefore, all that God does is right, and his very existence is right, for his existence is one and the same as his being God, the identity in distinction of his concept and his intuition.[71]

The Father is God as noumenon; the Son, as phenomenon; and the Spirit, as their identity. The persons are supreme ends in themselves, to produce intuitions of one another, who have their lawfulness within themselves. There must therefore be intuitions to make known the persons. These intuitions are the judgments executed upon Jesus Christ. That there should be a manifestation of God in the flesh, pertains to the Son of God, as the image of the invisible God; and in this revelation each person is revealed in a judgment upon the Son.

Therefore, the intuition he produces of himself, in accordance with his concept, is in his only begotten Son, the Lord Jesus Christ. In him, the identity of righteousness and blessedness thought in the divine nature, is

---

[70] Gen. 1:1, Ex. 3:14, 1 John 5:7, 10. Anselm was right; the existence of God can be demonstrated from the concept, but not as that than which nothing greater can be conceived, but as three persons subsisting in one divine nature. The non-existence, not of God, but of the Triune God is intrinsically contradictory.
[71] Col. 1:15-17; Heb. 1:2-3.

intuited in the distinction seen in the human nature, through the harmony of diverse judgments executed upon him, and therein the absolute unity of the divine nature is revealed, for it is one with God to justify and to condemn.

Theology begins with the Trinity. The existence of God, his nature and attributes, his works, his unity, invisibility, and visibility in Christ, his judgments, his works, and his glory, flow from the Trinity. The Trinity is the essence[72] of God.

---

[72] That whereby a thing is fully understood. The essences of things are other than their definitions, in agreement with them.

Conclusion

The purpose of this work is to show that salvation is possible through the Trinity, and the knowledge of the Trinity through the Incarnation. Salvation is a transition from a state of sin and misery into a state of righteousness and life. The divine nature condemns sin, and rewards it with misery and death; the divine nature justifies righteousness, and rewards it with happiness and life. Therefore, the possibility of salvation consists of the ground of a transition from condemnation to justification, for God does not change, yet the persons are three. We see this transition in Jesus Christ, and it is lawful for the sake of the divine persons revealed therein, for the divine persons are grounds of the possibility of divine judgments, and by them condemnation is transformed into justification.

Salvation must be received. To be lawfully received, it must be lawfully conceived. Salvation is lawfully conceived through the Trinity, and the divine persons are lawfully conceived through Jesus Christ, according to the judgments that reveal them. Wherefore, salvation is in the knowledge of the Trinity, and the end of salvation is the knowledge of the divine persons.[1]

The persons are necessary from the viewpoint of practical reason, as is the existence of God. The moral law prescribes an intuition to be produced. It commands men to persevere in original righteousness. Man having sinned, the moral law commands men to repent. Therefore, a sinner who seeks righteousness may no more dispense with the Incarnation and the Trinity, then he may with the immortality of the soul, the freedom of the will, or the existence of God.

The Incarnation and the Trinity are verified by theoretical reason, which uses the practical conception of the divine being to formulate an apodictic argument regarding the triune God. And the apodictic certainty of redemption satisfies the need of human reason, to conceive of a salvation that so greatly exceeds its natural capacity.

As nature reveals the existence of God in an aesthetic judgment, so also the word of God reveals the Incarnation and the Trinity. These doctrines may indeed be known through their conception, but the conception itself may only be given to man through revelation. And the revelation of

---

[1] Augustine, *Trinity* I.1.4.

divine mysteries is one of the incomparable excellencies of Scripture, whereby we know that it is the word of God.

Wherefore, the fundamental doctrines of the Christian faith are theoretically certain, practically necessary, aesthetically revealed. As man has no excuse for his sin, so also sinners have no excuse for their obstinacy. God calls men to repent of their sins and believe in Jesus Christ, for he is righteous in saving sinners, and the righteousness of his salvation is disclosed in the person of his Son, who shows us into "the bosom of the Father" (John 1:18).

> Seek ye the LORD while he may be found, call ye upon him while he is near: Let the wicked forsake his way, and the unrighteous man his thoughts: and let him return unto the LORD, and he will have mercy upon him; and to our God, for he will abundantly pardon. For my thoughts *are* not your thoughts, neither *are* your ways my ways, saith the LORD. For *as* the heavens are higher than the earth, so are my ways higher than your ways, and my thoughts than your thoughts. For as the rain cometh down, and the snow from heaven, and returneth not thither, but watereth the earth, and maketh it bring forth and bud, that it may give seed to the sower, and bread to the eater: So shall my word be that goeth forth out of my mouth: it shall not return unto me void, but it shall accomplish that which I please, and it shall prosper *in the thing* whereto I sent it. For ye shall go out with joy, and be led forth with peace: the mountains and the hills shall break forth before you into singing, and all the trees of the field shall clap *their* hands. Instead of the thorn shall come up the fir tree, and instead of the brier shall come up the myrtle tree: and it shall be to the LORD for a name, for an everlasting sign *that* shall not be cut off. Isaiah 55:6-13

METHOD

Method is the form of cognition.[1] The matter of cognition refers to an object, the method of cognition to the subject and to its conception of the object, whether this conception is understood according to quantity, quality, relation, or modality.[2] *Architectonic* refers to quantity of cognition, to the structure of concepts, wherein every universal contains others under it, or is contained under others above.[3] *Discipline* to the quality of cognition, to what it affirms or denies, and what sort of knowledge it yields, and insight with it.[4] *Canon* concerns the relation of that cognition to the ends of the rational being.[5] *History* concerns the relation of that cognition to the cognitive being in time, as the cognition is possible, actual, or necessary. Hence, the history of the doctrine will deal with the definition of terms, progression of concepts, and refutation of heresies.[6]

ARCHITECTONIC

Architectonic consists of the order and structure of concepts. One concept is subordinated to another, another to it. For any cognition, its place in the system may be given.

Theology concerns itself with the highest being. All concepts are thought through unity and affirmation. All things have their being through the spirit of affirmation.

It is the purpose of God that, as he himself is the spirit of affirmation, so also all other concepts and intuitions affirmed by him should subsist in rational beings, whose essences they are. All that is thought in God, is distributed to his individual creatures; and every individual perfection thought in the creature, is thought universally in God, in identity with the rest.[7]

The subordinate ends may only be conceived through persons, because each one falls under a genus, and no species may subsist under a genus without particularity. It follows that to every finite rational being,

---

[1] Kant, *Pure Reason*, B733-736; *Logic*, Sections 94-96.
[2] *Pure Reason*, Bxxii-xxiv; *Logic*, Sections 97-98, 107-108.
[3] *Pure Reason*, B860-863; Reich, *Completeness*, 37-39.
[4] Kant, *Pure Reason*, Bxxiv-xxx, B736-740.
[5] *Pure Reason*, Bxxx-xxxv, B823-829.
[6] *Pure Reason*, B880-884.
[7] Aquinas, *Summa* 1.4.2-3, 1.26.4, 1.44.1. Philosophy distinguishes, theology identifies.

man or angel, there is but one person, whose essence is one. However, affirmation is above all other concepts, and belongs to no genus; therefore, the divine nature may be conceived without a proper person, as the most universal being.[8]

Hence, the creation of the world is for the sake of the creature, not the Creator. God is indeed the supreme end of all things; all things are subject to him, and he rewards every man according to his works, but he is not yet an end in himself, for the divine persons are not known in the state of creation, only those reasonable creatures he has made.

Nevertheless, the end of redemption is the knowledge of the divine persons, who are revealed in the Lord Jesus Christ. Therefore, the doctrine of revealed religion conceives of the whole of creation as a system subject to the divine persons. Every man and angel is thought in relation to them, and exists not only for his own sake, but as a representation of the divine persons, for the glory of the Triune God. Hence, the creature is not merely a pattern of the divine nature, but an image; he bears the glory of God, and partakes of the divine nature through exceeding precious promises.[9]

The personal unity of the creature follows from the conception of his essence as subordinate to a genus. God's essence is affirmation, and affirmation belongs to no genus; it is original. Any persons in God must therefore be thought through pure a priori relations. There are three such relations, and therefore three divine persons, according to the threefold conception of his nature, as righteous, blessed, and holy.

There can be no application of the categories to things without an intuition;[10] and if such an intuition is provided, the categories must be employed for cognition.[11] Hence, the system of theology depends upon revelation.[12] God, having manifested himself in the Lord Jesus Christ, is known according to a system; and there is therefore an obligation to enumerate that system according to the human conception thereof.[13]

Theology is concerned with the highest being. Full understanding of the Creator may therefore be sought through knowledge of subordinate ends; and understanding of the system as a whole is attained through

---

[8] Aquinas, *Summa* 1.3.5, 1.32.1.
[9] 2 Pet. 1:4. Gen. 3:5; Lev. 11:44-45, 19:2, 20:26; Ps. 90:17; 2 Cor. 5:21; Jas. 1:19-20.
[10] Kant, *Pure Reason*, B146-148.
[11] *Pure Reason*, Bxvii-xviii, B143.
[12] Deut. 29:29; James 1:21.
[13] Eph. 4:1-16; Rev. 11:3-7.

knowledge of the Creator. In this way all things form a system reflecting the glory of the Creator. Hence our inquiry began with logic, and proceeded to critique, first of theoretical reason, then of practical, then of judgment, and finally of revelation. As men we begin with what is lowest, and ascend to the highest.[14] God begins with the highest, himself, in whom lies the pattern of all things made, for "he is the image of the invisible God, the firstborn of all creation," that in one full view one may understand the divine purpose of the world as lying in the holy Trinity from eternity past (Colossians 1:15).

The complete enumeration of concepts in their systematic connection is the labor of transcendental philosophy.[15] Theology is the system that explicates the nature of God, the divine persons, and their work. This system is above all others, that for the sake of which all others exist.[16]

The sum total of concepts and intuitions, so far as these inhere in persons, as their essences, is a body, wherein each one exists for the sake of the others, and all the others for it, as a representation of God himself, who is the ground of all things.[17]

> That in the dispensation of the fulness of times he might gather together in one all things in Christ, both which are in heaven, and which are on earth; *even* in him: In whom also we have obtained an inheritance, being predestinated according to the purpose of him who worketh all things after the counsel of his own will: That we should be to the praise of his glory, who first trusted in Christ. Ephesians 1:10-11

> Now therefore ye are no more strangers and foreigners, but fellowcitizens with the saints, and of the household of God; And are built upon the foundation of the apostles and prophets, Jesus Christ himself being the chief corner *stone*; In whom all the building fitly framed together groweth unto an holy temple in the Lord: In whom ye also are builded together for an habitation of God through the Spirit. Ephesians 2:19-22, cf. 1 Cor. 12:1-31, Eph. 3:14-15, Col. 1:16-17, 1 Pet. 2:4-6

---

[14] Aristotle, *Metaphysics* 993b8-11; *Nichomachean Ethics* 1095a30-1095b12.

[15] Kant, *Pure Reason*, B27-28, B107-108.

[16] Aristotle, *Metaphysics* A.1-2.

[17] Kant, *Pure Reason*, B606-608; *Judgment*, ak. 369-376.

DISCIPLINE

Discipline concerns the quality of cognition. This pertains to the object of knowledge, the character of the proofs, and the insight yielded by them.

Theology is the study of a being that lies beyond the realm of nature.[18] Speculative philosophy must therefore restrict itself solely to the theoretical conception of God, without postulating any being signified thereby.[19] Practical philosophy is, however, directed toward supernatural objects, and may therefore presuppose the existence of such a being as is required for man's moral purpose, without claiming any theoretical knowledge of this being. The third branch of philosophy, which belongs to judgment, shows how, in judgments concerning the beautiful and the sublime, man's moral purpose harmonizes with the world in which it is to be actualized. Man thereby acquires knowledge of God's existence, without any insight into his being.

The knowledge of God bequeathed to man through reason suffices for him to persevere in original righteousness. Man having sinned, that knowledge requires that he be punished. Wherefore, salvation depends upon a unique application of the judgment of God to sinners, but a distinct exercise of the divine nature is only possible through a person; hence, redemption requires knowledge of the divine persons. These persons may, in turn, only be given through their judgments upon a human being, in whom the divine nature is indirectly revealed, through the harmony of diverse judgments executed upon him.

Nevertheless, there are doctrines without which neither the revelation itself, nor the salvation offered would be possible. These same doctrines are taught in Scripture, and are to be demonstrated from Scripture. However, Scripture also gives the reasons of these doctrines according to a system, for the word of God is "engrafted" onto the reasonable souls of men, and there must not only be a system of reason in God, but also in men, whereby men are fit to receive the revelation of God (James 1:21). Therefore, the same doctrines are to be demonstrated from reason, and the reasons themselves made evident from Scripture, so that in all things we

---

[18] John 1:18; 1 Tim. 6:16; Kant, *Pure Reason*, B662-664.
[19] *Pure Reason*, B664-667.

attend not only to the truth of the proposition, but the reason of its truth, which is also truth.[20]

Theology concerns itself with a being that transcends the limits of human reason, who has yet revealed himself to us. Theology must therefore restrict itself to the revelation of God in Jesus Christ, for although the system of reason is complete within itself, it may yet be augmented if new intuition is provided to which reason may apply its principles.[21] Such new information may only be given in solution of a problem of reason's own, that is, human sin.[22] The new data capable of solving this problem is given through an experience, though indirect, of the divine nature, given in the Lord Jesus Christ, who is God manifest in the flesh. Reason, that is, human reason then receives something that did not grow from its own roots, but is engrafted onto it, the word of God, "which is able to save [men's] souls" (James 1:21).

Therefore, in the work of redemption, the knowledge of God is expanded. By it man obtains practical insight into the divine nature. Theoretical insight into the divine nature is only possible in a future angelic state, wherein man sees the divine nature.[23] Practical insight yields theoretical certainty through practical concepts of God; it constitutes insight into the divine nature, but only when used for practical purposes, and it suffices for fallen man to repent of his sins, and do his duty.[24]

Reason therefore receives a supernatural extension, an ability to deduce practical truths as are required for salvation, in dependence on revelation, for these doctrines have the peculiarity that, once conceived through revelation, they are knowable entirely a priori. The conception of them proves their truth, a conception that may only be lawfully obtained through revelation, but is apodictically necessary once received, because it contains insight into a self-existent being.[25] The system is prior to experience, and may be known through its concept, if the concept is given; yet it does not

---

[20] 1 Thess. 5:21.

[21] Kant, *Pure Reason*, Bxxi-xxii, B6-10.

[22] *Pure Reason*, Ax-xiii.

[23] Matt. 22:30; Mark 12:25; Luke 24:36.

[24] Deut. 29:29. Kant said, "I have therefore had to annul *knowledge* in order to make room for *faith*" (*Pure Reason*, Bxxx). It is, however, only necessary to limit knowledge, by affirming it, but denying insight. Nevertheless, in revealed religion, insight is possible, but it is again limited by the practical conception of God that gives rise to it, because men do not see the divine nature as such.

[25] John 3:18.

follow that revelation can be dispensed with afterwards, for it was always through revelation that the insight originally came to be.

And because of its apodictic truth, all conditions of its actuality are known apodictically as well. The creation of the world, and the fall of men, are conditions of the actuality of redemption from sin. Wherefore, the Incarnation and the Trinity give original insight into both, all things being subject to the divine persons, who are supreme ends in themselves. Though the Trinity is not discoverable without either the creation or the fall, yet once discovered through the work of redemption, the Trinity yields to both apodictic certainty, for without them the divine persons cannot be glorified in the work of redemption.

CANON

Canon concerns the relation of cognition to the ends of the rational being. These purposes consist of thought, action, and feeling.

The purpose of creation is the good of the creature, for in that state the divine persons are not known, and therefore the only ends with the grounds of their existence within themselves are subordinate. However, after sin enters the world, and God reveals himself through the promise of his Son, the final end of creation is known to be the glory of God. Although all things are subject to the divine being, they do not find in him the sufficient purpose of their existence, but only the necessary condition of their being, until they come to know the divine persons.

Once revealed, the rational being understands, not only his own nature, but his own person to proceed from the Trinity. He cognizes himself in relation to them, and even his righteousness as proceeding from them; for having fallen into sin, it is only through them that he may be redeemed.

Hence, the end of creation is the glory of God in the rational being. Those who partake of Christ, partake of God's righteousness, and of the divine nature.

In any study, the first is what is worthy in itself, and above all, what is supremely worthy in itself. The divine persons are the supreme ends in themselves; knowledge of them is the supreme end of all things. And therefore contemplation of them is the first end to which our knowledge of the persons must be directed. To know the persons, to contemplate them, is the highest end of the creature.

God reveals himself to man, not as an object of speculative reason, but of practical.[26] He is to be sought, not by the mere understanding of his nature, but by contemplation of the persons, as supreme ends in themselves, to be glorified through repentance from sin. Therefore, the second end to which our knowledge of the Trinity ought to be directed is the performance of all our duties, as from out of a state of sin, into a state of righteousness and peace.

In the contemplation of the persons, and the performance of good deeds flowing from them in us, man's happiness resides; for therein man's cognition is in harmony with his will. Man's holiness consists of a feeling of pleasure in his conformity to the divine nature. Man's happiness is not then in the good things of this world, but in the Lord alone,[27] of whose holiness man partakes. And thus men are made as happy as God himself.

> I say unto you, that likewise joy shall be in heaven over one sinner that repenteth, more than over ninety and nine just persons, which need no repentance. Luke 15:7

This joy is greater than the first, because it is equal to it and something more; to righteousness it adds the conversion from sin to righteousness, which is good and desirable, and in which consists man's conformity to the image of God's Son.[28]

Thus, full understanding of the divine nature is to be sought by contemplation of the divine persons, by the performance of good works, and by the enjoyment of holy affections. As we think upon the persons, we are sanctified by them, and as we are sanctified by them, we partake of holy affections from them, such grace and peace and truth as is everywhere offered in the Gospel. And these feelings further the good works done for their glory, and the contemplation of their persons.

---

[26] 1 Cor. 8:1-3, 13:8-13; Jas. 1:22.

[27] Ps. 73:25.

[28] Rom. 8:29. We may learn a lesson from the theory of music. *Consonance* means "sounding together," not "sounding good together," for what sounds together sounds good. *Dissonance* means "not sounding together," but what does not sound together by itself, may sound together with the whole; though dissonance is always dissonance, the resolution from dissonance to consonance is consonance. In God is the resolution of conflict without conflict.

In the state of creation, the law is indeed the determining ground of the will, and every rational creature is obliged to obey God out of respect for duty.[29] However, respect for law is not sufficient to determine the will only and forever to that which is good, but happiness will always be alongside it, as something besides. And therefore, man is susceptible to sin, and actually falls into sin, when tempted with the prospect that he may be as holy, and therefore as happy as God himself is. Yet, in the Gospel, the law is written in the heart of man,[30] and he obeys it, not only out of respect, but love. For having been saved from sin through the very law that ought to have destroyed him, he now longs to obey the law that God himself has magnified, and made honorable, for his good.[31] Whoso is forgiven much, loves much,[32] for Adam respected God's law, Jesus loved it.

> I delight to do thy will, O my God: yea, thy law *is* within my heart. Psalm 40:8

> O how I love thy law! it *is* my meditation all the day. Psalm 119:97, cf. Ps. 1:2, 19:10, 119:14, 16, 20, 35, 40, 47, etc.

HISTORY

The history of method refers to the modality of cognition. The possibility of cognition consists of the meaning of terms; actuality, its progress; necessity, the refutation of all heresies.

By history of method, I mean the history of the study of the doctrine, not of the doctrine itself. For the doctrine has no history, except in its manifestation in history, which doctrine pertains to the Son. The history of the doctrine considers not the object, but the subject, insofar as it comes to understand the doctrine over time.

I offer these guidelines to those who may exercise themselves in this field; as well as to those who seek a basic understanding of the history of the doctrine, and an illustration of the history of method.

The meaning of a term consists of definition, context, and usage. *Definition* is that affirmation of a thing that suffices to distinguish it from all

---

[29] Kant, *Groundwork*, 4:400-401; *Practical Reason*, 5:71-89.
[30] Jer. 31:33.
[31] Is. 42:21.
[32] Luke 7:36-50.

104

that it is not.[33] A literalist believes that the meaning of words may be determined solely from their definition. *Context* determines the author's appropriation of a word to his particular circumstances. There can be no meaning to a word, unless an author appropriates it. This appropriation may be analytic or synthetic. It is analytic when he relies solely upon the definition; synthetic, when he adds something to the definition, as in idioms and figures.[34] *Usage* is the sum total appropriation of a word by a community. Usage may either alter or modify the definition, magnify it and bring it to precision, or make technical use of the word by a specialized community.

The following words are commonly used in this study and require definition: substance, subsistence, inherence, essence, person, nature, accident. I will not here attempt a complete definition of them, for they sometimes vary, and I have appropriated them as I saw fit. By *substance* I understand the matter of a thing conceived as a universal predicate; *subsistence* the relation of a subject to its predicate; *inherence* the relation of a predicate to its subject; *essence* is that which explains why a thing is what it is; *person* is the subject of a moral nature; *nature* is the most universal predicate of a subject; and *accident* is the particular predicate thought under the nature.

The Old Testament concerns the constitution of concepts. The ideas of plurality within unity, and of legal states, are present within the law to an exceptional degree, in the form of sacrifices and types of Christ, and in laws, both ceremonial, and judicial, and the full exposition of those moral. In the New Testament, however, we find an abundance of the glory of the persons in their relations both to one another and to humanity. The Old Testament belongs to a nation constituted holy, wherein church and state are identified in distinction. The New Testament, however, reveals the grace itself with which this identity is concerned. Laws of cleanness, sacrifice, moral laws, judicial laws, etc., all reveal the division between right and wrong, life and death, and the harmony to be found in the Gospel. The Gospel, however, reveals the persons themselves, and their saving grace.

The clarification of the doctrine through definitions of words examines the history of doctrine in the church, consisting of councils and creeds. It bears some relation to the history of the world, and the universal plan of

---

[33] Kant, *Logic*, Section 99.
[34] *Pure Reason*, B10-11.

salvation, so it is omitted here, in the expectation that it will be more fully unveiled in a work on the history of redemption.

The refutation of heresies consists of tracing the development of the doctrine against all heresies. Rather than enumerating all the various objections, and refuting them by multitudes of reasons, either peculiar to each, or common to all; we may cut to the heart of the matter by first demonstrating the necessity of the doctrine for salvation, and its theoretical certainty, which is taught in Scripture; that we may more commodiously proceed to give our individual objections against each in the form of a system. For all knowledge must be united systematically, and the abundance of it catalogued by reason in such a way that one person may be able to comprehend it in one view, without excessive labor. A negative proposition, based on an affirmative, is derivative.[35] Full understanding must be sought first through the positive demonstration of doctrine; then the refutation of all heresies follows as a matter of course.

One must then follow the defense of them through the ages against all heresy, partly by tracing the types of heresies that arose over time, and partly by classifying those errors that have arisen. The latter is to be done by explicating heresies as violations of the law of non-contradiction, which either identify the divine and human natures of Christ, or distinguish his person from itself; or which identify the persons, or any of their properties, or distinguish the nature from itself, or any of its attributes.

Any doctrine that distinguishes the person of Christ from itself, or identifies the divine and human natures of Christ, or else identifies the persons of the Trinity, or distinguishes the divine nature from itself, violates the law of non-contradiction, and is heresy. Such a gospel cannot save.

---

[35] Kant, *Pure Reason*, B603.

WORKS CITED

Descartes, Rene. 1960. "The Meditations Concerning First Philosophy."
   In *Philosophical Essays*, translated by Laurence J. Lafleur. New
   York: Macmillan/Library of Liberal Arts.

Gress, Julian. 2018. *The Harmony of Reason and the Possibility of Man's Final
   End in Kant's Critique of Judgment.* Revised.
   juliangress.mywriting.network: Julian Gress.

Kant, Immanuel. 1987. *Critique of Judgment.* Translated by Werner S.
   Pluhar. Indianapolis: Hackett Publishing Company.

—. 1997. *Critique of Practical Reason.* Edited by Mary Gregor. Translated by
   Mary Gregor. Cambridge: Cambridge University Press.

—. 1996. *Critique of Pure Reason.* Translated by Werner S. Pluhar.
   Indianapolis: Hackett Publishing Company.

—. 1998. *Groundwork of the Metaphysics of Morals.* Edited by Mary Gregor.
   Translated by Mary Gregor. Cambridge: Cambridge University
   Press.

—. 1996. "Lectures on the philosophical doctrine of religion." In *Religion
   and Rational Theology*, edited by Allen W. Wood and George di
   Giovanni, translated by Allen W. Wood. New York: Cambridge
   University Press.

—. 1974. *Logic.* Translated by Robert S. Hartman and Wolfgang Schwarz.
   Mineola: Dover Publications.

—. 2004. *Metaphysical Foundations of Natural Science.* Edited by Michael
   Friedman. Translated by Michael Friedman. Cambridge:
   Cambridge University Press.

—. 1996. *Metaphysics of Morals.* Edited by Mary Gregor. Translated by
   Mary Gregor. Cambridge: Cambridge University Press.

—. 1996. "On the miscarriage of all philosophical trials in theodicy." In
   Religion and Rational Theology, edited by Allen W. Wood and
   George di Giovanni, translated by George di Giovanni. New
   York: Cambridge University Press.

—. 1993. *Opus postumum*. Edited by Eckart Forster. Translated by Eckart Forster and Michael Rosen. New York: Cambridge University Press.

—. 1950. *Prolegomena to Any Future Metaphysics*. Edited by Lewis White Beck. Translated by Paul Carus. New York: Macmillan/Library of Liberal Arts.

—. 1996. "Religion within the boundaries of mere reason." In *Religion and Rational Theology*, edited by Allen W. Wood and George di Giovanni, translated by George di Giovanni. New York: Cambridge University Press.

—. 1996. "What does it mean to orient oneself in thinking?" In *Religion and Rational Theology*, edited by Allen W. Wood and George di Giovanni, translated by Allen W. Wood. New York: Cambridge University Press.

Reich, Klaus. 1992. *The Completeness of Kant's Table of Judgments*. Edited by Eckart Forster. Translated by Jane Kneller and Michael Losonsky. Stanford, California: Stanford University Press.

Made in the USA
Middletown, DE
12 June 2023

32485383R00073